Longing for Love

Longing for Love

Justice Saint Rain

Book 3 of the
Love, Lust and the Longing for God trilogy,
which includes:
The Secret of Emotions
&
4 Tools of Emotional Healing

SPECIAL IDEAS

Special Ideas
511 Diamond Rd Heltonville IN 47436
1-800-326-1197

Longing for Love
By Justice Saint Rain

This book may be purchased individually at
Amazon.com or purchased both individually and in bulk at
www.secretofemotions.com or www.interfaithresources.com

Other books by Justice Saint Rain

The Secret of Emotions
4 Tools of Emotional Healing
Why Me? A Spiritual Guide to Growing Through Tests
The Secret of Happiness
A Spiritual Guide to Great Sex
Falling Into Grace
My Bahá'í Faith
The Hard Way – Lessons Learned
from the Economic Collaps

Printed in the USA

ISBN 978-188854753-5

To all of the people I thought I loved
but discovered I didn't,
and all the people I should have loved
but didn't know how to love.
And to my wife and children,
who help me understand love
a little more each day.

INTRODUCTION

This is book three in the series *Love, Lust and the Longing for God*. In the first book of this series, *The Secret of Emotions*, I explain that emotions are sensations that tell us about the attributes of God, or *virtues*, that we experience in our environment, and that love, in particular, is an attraction to these virtues.

An understanding of these two ideas, especially the second, is critical to any attempt to find true love and have healthy relationships. So this introduction will review these concepts.

What Emotions Are

Most of our actions are guided more by our emotions than our reason, and yet few people understand the nature of emotions or what emotional sensations are trying to tell us. We follow the promptings of our heart without understanding its language. In fact, the more sure we are that we know what we are feeling, the more likely it is that we are completely confused.

This is not our fault. How can we be expected to understand a language that neither we nor any of our family, friends or teachers have been taught?

In order to understand the language of the heart, I offer a simple observation:

The words associated with positive emotional sensations, such as hope, kindness, enthusiasm, gratitude, wonder and others, are also the words we use to name virtues.

In fact, here is a whole list of positive emotions named after the virtues that are present when we feel them:

Compassion	Grace	Nobility
Confidence	Gratitude	Optimism
Contentment	Happiness	Patience
Courage	Hope	Peace
Creative	Honesty	Perseverance
Determination	Humility	Radiance
Empathy	Initiative	Resilience
Enthusiasm	Integrity	Respect
Faith	Joy	Reverence
Forgiveness	Kindness	Serenity
Friendship	Love	Strength
Generosity	Loyalty	Wonder
Gentleness	Modesty	

Surrounding ourselves with these virtues, whether it is in the friends we keep or the qualities we practice, feels good. Conversely, when we are feeling a positive emotion, we are probably in the presence of a virtue. Our emotions are messengers that tell us about our spiritual environment.

Negative emotions, then, tell us when these virtues and others are absent. Anger tells us that we perceive a lack of justice. Fear tells us we lack security. Shame tells us that we were not treated with nobility. The feelings we carry with us from our childhood tell us the qualities that were missing in our early lives.

These feelings are messengers. Instead of clinging to them when they are good, or hiding from them when they are bad, we can learn from them. They tell us which virtues we love, and they tell us which virtues are missing.

What Love Is

Pieces of iron are innately attracted to a magnet. Flowers in a garden naturally turn towards the light of the sun. When we walk through that garden, we are instinctively drawn to bend down and smell the sweetness of a rose.

The heart is naturally attracted to the signs of God in the world. This attraction—this innate tendency to turn, towards beauty, kindness, enthusiasm and generosity—is the essence of love.

When we look around the world, the best reflections of these qualities can be found in the human soul.

Human love, then, is simply the recognition of, admiration for and attraction to the attributes of God in another person.

This attraction is felt in the heart. It is warm and pleasant, and grows with increased interaction. It is rarely overwhelming, and can be felt for people of any age, race or sex.

If we have learned to love such attributes as kindness, patience, responsibility, and joyfulness, then we will recognize, appreciate and be attracted to these qualities when we see them expressed in a human being—no matter who the person may be.

How much we love a person is determined by our ability to recognize virtues when we experience them, the strength of our attraction to those virtues, and the number and quality of virtues that the person expresses.

Take a look at that definition again. It is simple and universal, but it may contradict your long-held beliefs about love. You may, for example, want to separate love into several sub categories like romantic love, brotherly love and parental love. Or you may want to define love by the things we do as a result of feeling love—things like psychologist Erich Fromm's care, responsibility, respect and knowledge from his book *The Art of Loving*, or Scott Peck's the will to extend oneself for the purpose of nurturing one's own or another's spiritual growth. You might associate love with many of the intense feelings that masquerade as love, such as passion, attachment or need.

This book's definition of love focuses on a person's qualities rather than his or her personality, and on our attraction to those qualities rather than the actions that are the result of that attraction. What does it mean to be attracted to a quality rather than a person? Let's take as examples two of the qualities I've been mentioning: kindness and responsibility.

Experiencing someone's kindness generates a sensation. It feels good just to watch a person showing kindness, even if it is towards someone else. If we are attracted to kindness—if we see it as a sign of strength instead of weakness—then our attraction will also generate a sensation. It feels like the invisible pull of a magnet. When the sensation of attraction combines with the sensation of kindness, they reinforce one another to a point that it is impossible to ignore or dismiss. The strength of the combined sensation can spill over into a general positive regard for the person expressing this attractive virtue.

The virtue of responsibility also generates sensations. Watching a person make wise and thoughtful decisions in the face of temptations to do otherwise can be very uplifting, and yet not as many people are aware of these sensations because they have not been taught to recognize and be attracted to them. Without the attraction, the sensations go unnoticed and are not reinforced. They therefore do not spill over into a general appreciation for the person demonstrating responsibility. If we don't love the qualities a person demonstrates, it is difficult to feel that we love them, no matter how wonderful they may be.

It is our ability to be attracted to positive qualities, then, that expands our ability to love the people around us. This means that the more virtues we learn to recognize and be attracted to, the more people we will love, and the more rewarding our interaction with them will be.

The second book in this series, *Four Tools of Emotional Healing* is about four specific virtues that can help heal the most common sources of emotional pain. They replace the pain of shame, anger, loneliness and fear with honesty, forgiveness, compassion and faith. At the same time, they lay the foundation for many other virtues and the positive emotional sensations that go with them. I will mention these virtues several times in this third book, but you don't need to read the second book to know that they are valuable character traits to develop.

The goal of this third book is to expand our ability to recognize and become attracted to virtues so that we fall in love with people who are ready to have healthy, nurturing relationships. We will take a look at what these ideas look like when applied to finding and building healthy relationships in the real world.

How does our understanding of the relationship between emotions and virtues help us find healthy people to be friends with?

How does understanding the difference between love and lust change the way we enter into sexual relationships?

How do we tell the difference between the sensation of love and all of the other sensations that are generated by relationships?

How do we maintain healthy relationships once we commit to them?

How do we avoid temptations that can destroy the relationship we have?

These are the questions that we will be exploring in this third book. If you are unsure of the answers, then you are at the right place.

Acknowledgements

Many thanks to the people who read early copies of this work and gave invaluable feedback: Phyllis Edgerly Ring, editor, and the author of *Life at First Sight – Finding the Divine in the Details*; Phyllis K. Peterson, author of *Remaining Faithful*; Kim Bowden-Kerby, whose advice was worth much more than I paid for it; and Jay Cardwell who found more in it than I put in.

Thanks, also, to all of the readers of my earlier works whose support and encouragement made the publication of this book possible. I'm particularly grateful to the many readers at GoodReads.com whose enthusiastic reviews reassured me that I could make a difference in the lives of people whom I have never met.

Retraining Your Heart

The problem with most relationship guides is that they assume that we are rational people and then give us rational advice as to how to attract another rational person.

But we aren't rational. If we were, life would be much easier, but our behavior doesn't often proceed from our logical minds—no matter how much we may want to believe that it does.

The way that most people find their life partner is to find someone they are attracted to, enter into a relationship, and THEN, if the relationship gets serious, go through a checklist of qualities that they would like their spouse to have, in order to see if the relationship has potential.

If you want to have a healthy relationship, you must do the exact opposite of this.

By exact opposite, I don't mean that you should start by finding someone you are NOT attracted to. I mean that you should do these things in the reverse order.

Start by figuring out what qualities a person needs to have in order to be a healthy life-partner. The virtues from book two, which are Honesty, Forgiveness, Compassion and Faith in the general goodness of the universe, are a good place to start.

The next step is to train your heart to *recognize* these qualities when you encounter them.

Finally, with very little effort, you can retrain your heart to be *attracted* to these qualities when you see them expressed in the people you meet.

Please note that I am not suggesting that you force your head to override your heart. I am, instead, saying that your head can *train* your heart so that your heart and head can work together to create wonderful, nurturing, and long-lasting relationships.

The reason why it doesn't work to try to build relationships in the usual order is that if your heart is attracted to emotionally unhealthy people, then your heart will blind you to the absence of the qualities that you are looking for. Love is not blind, but the untrained heart sees what it wants to see, whether it is there or not. Train the heart first, and it will see accurately, and love truly.

Why we need to retrain our hearts

If our hearts keep leading us astray, we have three options:

We can stop listening to our hearts and live our lives in our heads.

We can resign ourselves to a life of chaos and heartbreak.

Or, we can retrain our hearts to give us accurate guidance.

What does it mean to retrain our hearts?

In *The Secret of Emotions*, I explain that our hearts, the center of our emotions, respond to the presence and absence of virtues. The problem is not that our hearts are faulty, but that 1) we have not taught them to look for the right things, and 2) we have misunderstood the sensations they have generated.

Retraining, then, involves both learning and unlearning—teaching our hearts how to recognize and become attracted to the sensations created in the presence of virtues and noble character traits, and unlearning our attraction to unhealthy sensations. This unlearning involves being able to correctly identify the sensations we are feeling, and overcoming our culture's fascination with the sensations of lust and intensity at the expense of love and intimacy.

In *The Secret of Emotions*, I explained how our emotional sensations are generated by the presence of virtues. Now I would like to revisit this idea from the perspective of the need to train our perception. Unless we understand how our hearts have been trained to recognize and respond to virtues up until now, we can't appreciate the need to retrain them so that we can recognize and respond in a healthier manner.

Hearts are Trained to Perceive Virtues

When we are born, we spend the first five or six years training our physical senses to accurately identify a wide variety of sensations. First we learn what hunger and pain feel like. Then heat and cold. Eventually we are given names for these sensations, and learn to make ever-finer distinctions. Cold, cool, normal, warm, and hot each take on subjective meaning. Oval, circle, square; sweet, sour, salty; blue, green, purple; children take delight in demonstrating to adults their mastery of these ever more subtle sensory distinctions. Eventually we can be trained to distinguish between musical notes, the letters "b" and "p" and even the smell of roses versus lilacs. While some of the sensory training we go through is simply a labeling process, much of it actually allows us to sense distinctions that would have been invisible to us without the training. Musicians train themselves to hear subtle variations in pitch, cooks can determine what spices are in similar foods, and artists can pick from maroon, burgundy, wine, plum, purple and violet. Publishers can tell you what typestyle this book is printed in. The ability to make these subtle distinctions in sensations requires time, training and practice.

In a very real sense, our physical survival depends upon our ability to distinguish between the sensations that signal health and safety and those that signal dangerous, disgusting or diseased input. Our instincts supply us with some of this knowledge, but much of it is only available as a result of conscious training. Our physical senses and the sensations they produce are a gift from God that allows us to function in the physical world.

Physical sensations are also a source of pleasure. The sweetness of an apple, the touch of a cool breeze on a cheek, the smell of cinnamon rolls in the oven. Sensations are much more delicate than is absolutely required for survival. They help us to discover the reflection of spiritual qualities in the material world.

The reason I am rambling on so long about the beauty, subtlety and value of physical sensations is to reintroduce the idea that emotions are *spiritual sensations.* I explored the broad implications of this idea in *The Secret of Emotions.* Now I want to look at it more deeply within the context of *relationships* and our ability to *train our hearts.*

While we train our children to identify *physical* sensations, we fail to train children in the identification of *spiritual* sensations, which leaves our hearts unable to accurately identify our emotions or the spiritual qualities present in the people we meet.

If God has been so kind and loving as to give us the physical senses we need in order to both survive in and enjoy the material world, would it not be logical to think that God would give us a set of spiritual senses that would enable us to survive in and enjoy the spiritual world as well? We are both physical and spiritual beings. Our physical reality consists of our bodies and our senses, while our spiritual reality consists of our souls and our virtues. Just as our physical senses tell us about the condition of our body and its physical surroundings, our spiritual senses tell us about the condition of our soul and the spiritual virtues that surround us.

This understanding of the heart as a perceptive tool of the soul that responds to virtues provides several useful perspectives in our quest for healthy relationships.

First, it gives us some useful questions to ask when we find ourselves in an emotional situation.

What is this sensation?
Where am I feeling it—in my heart or in my body, or both?
In what other situations have I experienced this sensation?
Can I identify an emotion associated with it?
What virtues might be associated with this sensation/emotion?
Are these reasonable virtues to associate with this situation?
Could this sensation be caused by a misreading of the situation?
What virtues could I apply in this situation to change my response to it?
What virtues could I apply in order to increase my enjoyment of it?

Asking these kinds of questions allows us to train our hearts to recognize and respond to virtues more effectively. This is not an instantaneous process. We do not go from being blindly buffeted by our emotions to self-control and development overnight. Awareness of the process is helpful, but it does not replace time and effort. Making a conscious effort to ask questions about our emotional responses might seem too difficult, too contrived, too analytical for real life. Yet we ask similar questions when we try to improve our understanding of other parts of our lives.

You might gain an appreciation for the process and the questions outlined above by relating them to the process of becoming a master chef. Think of emotions as being flavors and virtues as being spices. Most of us eat dozens of different foods every day and have a general idea of what flavors we enjoy, but very few of us understand or appreciate the complex interplay between base ingredients, spices, leavening, temperature, texture, etc. that makes the difference between edible food and aesthetic food. Wave a spice bottle under my nose and I can identify garlic, pepper, cinnamon, clove, mint and half a dozen other favorite spices. But with training and a love for the art of food, a person can learn to taste one bite of a dish and tell you exactly what ingredients are used and in what proportion—as well as making suggestions as to what spices might be added to make it even better. While most of us have a flavor palate of a dozen tastes, an expert can choose from hundreds of unique spices and ingredients so that every meal of every day is a new and wonderful experience.

Just for fun, let me rewrite the questions about spiritual sensations as though they were about food:

What is this sensation?

How am I feeling it—taste, texture, on my tongue, through the smell?

In what other foods have I experienced this sensation?

Can I identify a flavor associated with it?

What spices might be associated with this flavor?

Are these reasonable spices to associate with this type of food?

Could this flavor be caused by an unusual combination of ingredients?

What spices could I apply to this food to change my response to it?

What spices could I apply in order to increase my enjoyment of it?

Our culture's move towards fast food and pre-packaged meals has impoverished our ability to identify and appreciate excellence in the art of food preparation. Our culture's shaming of emotions and obsession with physical rather than spiritual pleasure has impoverished our ability to identify and appreciate the breathtaking beauty of our spiritual reality.

We can think of our spiritual sensations the same way as we think about our physical sensations, and train our heart the way a chef trains his palate. But train it to do what?

We train it to identify and respond more positively to virtues.

In other words, we *teach it how to love God*.

For some of us, the phrase "teaching our heart how to love" sounds blasphemous. Shouldn't we just listen to our hearts, and not try to tell them what to feel? Well, in a way we are. The heart, like your tongue, will taste whatever is there. It is our job to learn how to identify and appreciate the right things.

For example, most people don't like the taste of beer, whisky or cigarettes the first time they taste them. Our culture tells us, however, that these are tastes that "mature" people acquire, so, given time, many of us override our initial response and cultivate a taste for things that our bodies have correctly identified as unhealthy. Similarly, as children, we often have very clear and strong emotional reactions to certain situations. Observing cruelty, for example, often makes children cry. Given time, however, we can shame, ridicule and retrain children to enjoy the abuse of other children and become numb to the abuse of themselves. By the time we are adults, we have already had our hearts trained. But do we want to follow the guidance of our current training, or do we want to retrain ourselves to respond in more loving, healthy ways?

It is not too late

Is It Possible *to Retrain Our Hearts?*

Just as an adult palate can be trained to truly *enjoy* healthy foods, we can train our hearts to recognize and truly *love* healthy character traits. While it is true that some people will never like brussels sprouts, *everyone* can develop a taste for a wide range of properly prepared healthy foods. How could it be otherwise? If humans couldn't recognize and enjoy the taste of healthy food, we would have all died out eons ago.

Likewise, if our souls could not recognize and become attracted to the attributes of God when reflected in the character and actions of the people around us, the human race would not be able to fulfill its role in creation.

We were *created* with an innate longing for God, and that longing can best be fulfilled when we allow ourselves to become attracted to Divine Virtues when they are manifested in our own souls and in the people around us.

There are those who will say that it is impossible to change our attractions, but if that were true, then not only are we all doomed to unhealthy relationships, but the very foundation of religion is a sham.

The purpose of religion is to teach us how to love God— that is, to recognize and be attracted to God's qualities. If that is what we were created for, then it is irrational to think that we cannot teach ourselves how to do it. If we can't learn how to be attracted to the attributes of God in our primary relationships—the people we will spend our daily lives with—then when, where and how else will we do it? What good does it do to love God in the abstract if we are unable or unwilling to do it in the concrete here and now?

How I Discovered My Attractions Could Change

When I was in college to study art, I liked to think that I was attracted to beauty and repelled by ugliness. Why would I want to retrain myself? Shouldn't I just go by intuition? My teachers, I thought, should just teach me how to get my vision down on canvas, not try to retrain my vision.

Early in my freshman year, I was working in the pottery studio, throwing a cup, when I looked at a poster on the wall. It pictured a Japanese bowl that was brown, lopsided and cracked. I thought, "Why on earth would someone spend good money to produce a full-color poster of such an ugly bowl?" I was taking a class in Japanese art and culture that semester, but it was out of curiosity rather than a desire to emulate their style.

Three months later, I was back in the pottery studio when I happened to glance up at the wall. "My God, what a beautiful bowl!" I thought to myself—and then realized that it was the exact same poster that I had found so disgusting just a few months earlier.

Please note, *and this is important,* when I glanced up at that bowl, my automatic response was a heart-response, not an intellectual appreciation. I was not *thinking* about how pretty the bowl was, I was *feeling* an attraction to its innate beauty. Also, in this second instance, I had not set out to fall in love with a brown, lopsided, cracked bowl. I had not convinced myself that I *should* find it pretty, nor had the bowl changed in any way. I was the one who had been changed by the simple fact that I had opened myself up to another culture. I had not consciously chosen to find beauty in Japanese pottery, but I *had* consciously chosen to expose myself to a new way of looking at the world. In doing so, I had increased the range of "visual virtues" that I was capable of responding to.

The point of this story is not that you should learn to appreciate cracked Japanese bowls. The point is that *through exposure,* we can train our hearts to be attracted to those things that we *want* them to be attracted to—the virtues that will make us and our relationships nurturing and healthy.

Once we accept the idea that *what we love* is not determined by *fate* or set in *stone,* we can take control of and responsibility for the promptings of our heart. We can choose what we expose our hearts to. We can open ourselves up to healthy people and behaviors. Because these virtues are expressions of our true nature, with enough time and enough exposure, we *will* become attracted to them, and we *will* find that they bring great joy into our lives.

This brings us to three critical questions:

What virtues or character traits do we want to train ourselves to become attracted to?

How do we recognize them when we see them?

And *where* do we go to experience them in a safe environment so that we can open ourselves up to them and learn about them?

Let me start with some basics.

I'm going to assume that you are reading this book not so that you can go out and have a string of one-night-stands, but because you would like to enter into a long-term family-style relationship.

With that goal in mind, there are a number of virtues or character traits that it will be important for you to learn how to recognize and be attracted to that otherwise might not be high on your list of priorities. Likewise, some qualities that are very important in a fling or trophy relationship may not be important at all. Good looks, hot body, expensive car, fashion sense, a biting sense of humor, even a captivating public persona all become irrelevant when it comes time to change a diaper in the middle of the night.

So what qualities *are* important? The four I described at length in *4 Tools of Emotional Healing* are critical: honesty, forgiveness, compassion and faith (in *something*), along with responsibility, attentiveness, patience, listening skills, humility, confidence, optimism, courage, joy and many more. Picture yourself ten, twenty and thirty years in the future, possibly with children, probably with rent or mortgage payments, possibly health issues, dealing with all of the challenges that life throws at you. What kind of person do you want to spend your days with? What kind of person do you want to *be* in the future?

Thinking about these virtues, it is fairly obvious that jumping from romance to romance is *not* the best way to learn about them. These qualities are best observed in intimate friendships—especially with people who are *not* romantically available to you. Hanging out with people who are already married, are older or younger, or are otherwise unavailable gives you the opportunity to observe objectively.

You might be surprised at how much you can see when you aren't jockeying into a romantic position.

Watching a group, even from across a room, you can see who talks and who listens. Is the speaker engaging or boasting? Are the listeners attentive or waiting for a chance to jump in? When they laugh, are they laughing at others or with others? Do they radiate confidence or vanity, humility or shame? Do they encourage others or put them down? Do they look nervous? Do they smile, and is it real?

Study people.

Some virtues are amazingly easy to identify once you step back and watch rather than trying to impress or seduce the people you meet. Other times, vices masquerade as virtues and it takes time, attention and insight to tell the difference.

Open your heart, but don't assume that you understand what your heart is telling you. Pay attention. Your heart will respond to both the presence and the *absence* of virtues, so just because your heart is moved by someone does *not* mean that they are expressing a virtue that you want to spend your life with. If your heart responds to that nervous person, that does *not* mean that insecurity is a virtue, but rather that you are accustomed to associating love with rescuing people. If your heart beats faster when you hear a snarky laugh from across a crowded room, that does *not* mean you are enchanted, it means that you recognize cruel laughter and it scares you.

Hanging out with friends gives us the opportunity to study virtues, but we really *don't* want to develop intimate friendships with dishonest, judgmental or cruel people. Unfortunately, most of us don't know how to recognize these qualities in a person until after it is too late.

In the physical world, we are carefully taught the difference between dolphins and sharks, even though our chances of meeting either is fairly slim. But spiritually, we are introduced to sharks every day and are expected to ignore any spiritual sensations that might indicate danger. Indeed, we are often told that these people are exciting, suave or hard workers, thus associating positive virtues with the spiritual sensation of fear. But when we open our hearts to them, we find cruelty, deceit and selfishness.

Stock brokers, for example, are often considered smart, hard-working, good providers, with an admirable desire to get ahead. They would be considered a "great catch" and a good choice for a friend. A Swiss university, however, discovered that the stock brokers *they* studied (there are exceptions, of course) took more risks, were more manipulative and more focused on damaging their competitors than a control group of convicted psychopaths. In this case, what we called "smart" was really arrogant, "hard-working" was really workaholic, "good providers" meant materialistic and a "desire to get ahead" was actually cutthroat competitiveness.

If our hearts told us to be frightened of such a person, our minds (and our friends) would tell us we were wrong.

Because our hearts have been fooled so many times, we have trained ourselves not to respond too quickly or feel too deeply when meeting a new person. Our fear of being hurt or overwhelmed by unpleasant sensations has caused us to shut down our spiritual sensors almost entirely. We are, spiritually speaking, holding our breath in order to avoid the stench of the moral swamp we are living in. This response is perfectly reasonable, but it is emotionally stifling.

What we need is a way to know when it is safe to let our guard down and respond to a person. In other words, we need to know how to identify a person's virtues with our minds *before* we open our hearts too wide.

There are two steps to this, one emotional and one intellectual. Emotionally, we need to learn that it is OK to experience emotional sensations without naming them or acting on them. Intellectually, we need to increase our vocabulary so that we can eventually identify virtues when we see them and find the right name for them when we feel them.

Our culture has called many vices virtues and taught us to name many things "love" and "attraction" that really aren't. When we are too quick to try to identify a strong feeling, we can fall into the trap of believing we are attracted to a person or quality when we are not. I will describe some of the many sensations that we mistake for love later on in this book, but for now what I encourage you to say to yourself as you explore the relationship between virtues and emotional sensations is this:

"When I am in this situation, have this experience or am with this person, I experience a strong sensation that I feel compelled to integrate into my emotional vocabulary."

This lets you be "open to the unknown" without pushing you to respond in any particular direction or take any specific action. *Not* taking action gives us time to observe and study.

We observe what is going on with our minds and then we compare what we see with what we feel in our hearts. Over time, we will be able to correlate our emotional sensations with our intellectual understanding of virtues and name our feelings accurately.

Or, put another way, if we pay close attention, we can get our knowledge of virtues and our experience of virtues to line up and make sense. Then we will be able to use our emotions to tell us about the virtues we see in the people around us. We will also be able to use our minds to tell our hearts what our emotional sensations really mean.

When our hearts and our minds agree on what they see, and what they see is *good*, then we can feel safe and confident opening ourselves up to true intimate friendship. When we are sure that what we are perceiving is happy laughter, not cruel laughter, is compassionate sharing, not codependent complaining, is kindness, not manipulation, then we are on our way to developing the skills and the virtues that will attract intimate friends and lifetime companions into our lives.

Before we can get to this happy place, however, we must actually make an effort to learn about virtues with our minds. How do we do that? Where do we go to learn the names and descriptions of virtues so that our minds know what it is we should be looking for?

Four Tools for Identifying Virtues

A *Religious Approach to Identifying Virtues*

The first thing we need is a new vocabulary. One of the best places to learn the names and descriptions of virtues is in religious scripture. Though the world's religions rarely agree on theology or dogma, they all extol the value of virtues, and they do it in a language that is poetic and inspiring.

The stories, lessons, prayers and examples that can be found in the Holy Scriptures of the world's religions provide helpful tools in identifying, naming, appreciating and practicing the virtues that God wants us to develop.

When Jesus said, "Blessed are the peace makers," He was naming a virtue. When King David sang, "Justice and judgment are the habitation of Thy throne: mercy and truth shall go before Thy face," he was exalting virtues.

Religions help us define virtues by providing us with the names and descriptions of the virtues that God wants us to develop. You will not find these virtues in your economics classes, sports commentary or studies of animal behavior. They do not include good looks, material wealth or power over others. Some—like meekness and selflessness—are completely counter-intuitive and at cross-purposes with our cultural expectations. There is a reason why God's Messengers were rejected by the people of Their time. They were calling us to adopt virtues and behaviors that people really didn't want to practice—things like *turning the other cheek*. But the virtues of God's Messengers are the virtues that our hearts were created to reflect. They are expressions of our true spiritual nature and are, therefore, the ones that will ultimately lead to our happiness.

Scripture does something else with its description of virtue: it inspires us. Reading the definitions of virtues from a dictionary might give you a more precise description, but reading the stories, proverbs, songs and poems of the world's great religions helps us integrate our intellectual and spiritual understanding of virtues. Our hearts are moved while our minds are expanded. We do more than *learn* about virtues, we *long* for them. Verses like *"Surely goodness and mercy shall follow me all the days of my life,"* make us hope for life-long friends who would be good and merciful. Scripture may even help us imagine becoming good and merciful ourselves.

As we learn to identify virtues by studying the Holy Writings of the world's religions, we then have to look around us and try to recognize what they might look like in real life. It's like seeing a picture of a rose in a book, then finding one growing in a garden. The Holy Books describe virtues so that we will be better able to recognize them when we see them.

When you read scripture with an open heart and an open mind, your heart trains your mind to identify the virtues that move it emotionally. With practice, your mind can then help your heart identify when it is safe to open up in your personal relationships.

The Twelve-Step Approach to Identifying Virtues

When people think of twelve-step groups, they think that they are about quitting some behavior, but much of the sharing that goes on is not about the addiction, but about the virtues needed to kick the addiction—virtues like humility, strength, hope, forgiveness, compassion, service, detachment and faith. At meetings you will hear stories about these virtues, and witness people putting them into practice. Virtues take on a concrete quality as we watch them transform people's lives right before our eyes.

In church, virtues are a way to get you into heaven *when you die*. In recovery, virtues *keep you alive*. It is that simple and that stark. It is not about sweetness and light. Virtues are the weapons we use to fight our personal demons.

The other benefit of studying virtues in a twelve-step setting is that it gives us opportunities to practice making friends that are emotionally intimate without being sexually intimate. We see virtues being practiced by people of all ages and both genders. It helps us fine-tune our emotional compass.

The recovery community also uses affirmations to counteract the negative self-talk that many of us engage in. Many of these affirmations incorporate the names and descriptions of virtues that the recovery community has found to be useful in building healthy lives and relationships.

Using Our Life Experience to Identify Virtues

Now that you have a larger vocabulary of virtues from scripture, and have heard them talked about and seen them practiced in the recovery community, you can take what you've learned and go digging into your own life experience to uncover more examples of virtues and the emotional sensations they have generated.

Every relationship we can remember is an opportunity to learn something about what virtues look like. Instead of labeling relationships as good or bad, we can use our powers of discernment, combined with 20/20 hindsight to identify the virtues that each person did or did not have.

Were they kind? Honest? Generous? Supportive? Gentle? Creative? What is our evidence? What virtues did we *think* they had when we began the relationship? Why did we think that? What virtues did we see at the *end* of the relationship? If they weren't the same, how did we get fooled? What sensations did we experience when we first met? What did we *think* those sensations were telling us, and were we right? Can we now identify those sensations more accurately?

Are there patterns to what we are attracted to, and the ways we are fooled or confused? Do we often mistake pretty for sweet? Do we mistake wealthy for generous or arrogant for confident?

Now turn those questions around. How did we treat the people we were with? Were *we* kind, supportive, confident and loving? Do we mistake bossy for helpful, or needy for loving? What virtues could we have practiced to make the relationship more successful?

The goal of these questions is not to beat ourselves up for our relationship errors, but to mine gems of understanding from the most detailed and complete source of information we have access to—our own lives. If we are willing to look and ready to learn, then we can make our current and future relationships richer, more intimate, and more enjoyable.

Using Great Literature to Explore Virtues

While many characters in pulp fiction are two-dimensional, there are also some profoundly memorable characters, both good and bad, who exemplify the presence or absence of virtues. If we are moved by a story, we can be sure that there are virtues being explored. We can be passive readers (or viewers), or we can think deeply about why characters make the choices they do, what they might be feeling, and what this says about their character. As long as you remember that these are *imaginary* characters and don't go looking for your own princess or hero, you can learn a lot from literature.

Our Love Affair with Lust

So that was easy.

In order to have happy, healthy relationships, you simply stop looking for a relationship, then go out and learn how to recognize and become attracted to the virtues that make long-term healthy relationships possible. Once your heart is trained to love these virtues instead of being moved by shallow characteristics or imitation love, then you will only fall in love with mature, healthy people.

Now that you know how to do it right, you will never be tempted to fall for the wrong type of person again.

Right.

It is not enough to know how to create healthy relationships. You need to see the *whole* picture. That means that you need to recognize the sensations and behaviors that have led you into *unhealthy* relationships. These are the things you need to *unlearn*. Unless we discuss some of your old habits and why they don't work, and how to avoid temptations, and how they came to be accepted as normal behavior, you are likely to fall right back into old patterns. Recovery groups don't just talk about how great it is to be sober; they talk about all the things that might cause people to slide back into addiction.

This section, then, will explore some of the many emotional sensations that we mistake for love, and why the things that masquerade as love will lead us astray in the end.

In *The Secret of Emotions*, I explained that the sensations that are most often mistaken for love are a combination of fear, shame and lust. This mix of sensations creates the sweaty palms, racing heart, weak knees and tingling groin that many people interpret as a sign from God that they have finally met their soul mate.

The belief that these intense sensations are signs of love is almost universal in our culture. If we want to have any hope of having a healthy relationship based on love instead of shame, fear and lust, then this mythology is one of the first things we will need to unlearn. We need to unlearn the belief, and, even more difficult, we need to unlearn the behaviors that our culture has taught us are the right and natural expressions of that belief.

Simply *knowing* that there is a difference between shame and love gives us the opportunity to make a choice, but it doesn't make the choice for us. If we were to ask our hearts if we wanted our relationships to be built upon love or shame, our hearts would surely say *love*. In the real world, however, it is often our bodies that make decisions for us without our consent. In the world of physical sensation, the choice is experienced as being between intimacy and intensity.

In the long run, intimacy—and the love that makes it possible—is the more rewarding and healthy choice to make, but in a moment of passion, intensity makes a pretty convincing argument.

This chapter, then, is my attempt to explain the difference between intimacy and intensity, show why they are mutually exclusive, and offer arguments for why you should let your mind and heart override the impulses of your body so that you can have long-term healthy, loving and intimate relationships.

Intensity

Strong negative emotions, such as fear, shame and anger cause your body to release adrenaline and other stimulating hormones that create a state of physical arousal that I am calling intensity. It is a form of "fight or flight" response, which means that your senses are put on high-alert and your body is given extra energy to respond. Your heart beats faster, your palms sweat, you may feel weak in the knees, and your whole body seems to "buzz."

With your body in a state of hyper-sensitivity, sexual activity can be ecstatic, overpowering and exhausting. When movies depict wild passionate sex, this is the experience they are trying to capture.

This kind of sex might feel powerful and overwhelming, but does it feel *loving?* Jumping out of an airplane, riding a wave or skiing down a mountain may be exhilarating, but they have nothing to do with being attracted to a person's spiritual qualities.

If all of these powerful sensations are the byproduct of fear, shame or anger, then how can they be used as the foundation of a loving relationship?

The fact is, they can't. Fear, shame and anger are the opposite of trust, love and intimacy.

Fear is a sensation that tells us that the person we are with is dangerous. Shame is a flash of awareness that tells us that we are moving away from the qualities that we love. Anger tells us that we are being treated unfairly.

It is impossible to feel fear, shame and anger at the same time as we experience attraction, trust, openness, intimacy, safety and well-being.

So if we want to enjoy having sex with a safe, loving, supportive and appropriate partner, we will need to replace our fascination with intensity with an appreciation for intimacy.

Intimacy

Love is a light that never dwelleth in a heart possessed by fear.
— *Bahá'u'lláh*

Fear, shame and anger generate sensations because they warn us of the *absence* of the virtues of safety, nobility and justice.

Intimacy is a virtue that is built upon the *presence* of these virtues, so it also generates a sensation. It feels safe, warm and affirming, and it increases in strength over time.

If we think of intense sex as a shot of whiskey, we could describe intimate sex as a warm cup of hot chocolate.

Whiskey goes down quick. It burns. It creates a buzz and it helps you forget whatever it is you are trying to forget. It is very intense, but not necessarily pleasant, and if you want the sensation to last, you will have to keep throwing back those shots.

Hot chocolate is warm and soothing comfort food. It is sweet, it has chocolate to release pleasure endorphins, yet it also has some protein, calcium and carbohydrates to nourish you. Just the smell of it—the *thought* of it, you might say—can bring a smile to your lips. You wrap your hands around it, sip it slowly, feel its warmth for hours, and remember every moment of it. You can also drink it every night without becoming addicted or ill.

We teach ourselves to drink whiskey; to find that whisper of sweetness underneath the overpowering burn of the alcohol so that we can experience the buzz and the forgetting that goes with it. We are told that intense sex is the best sex there is.

We can also teach ourselves to become connoisseurs of the sweeter things of life. We can *choose* to make the deeper, sweeter, more enduring sensations of intimacy the ones we strive for. We just can't do both at the same time.

This Is the Choice

Because they are mutually exclusive, you can choose a fear and shame-based relationship with the drug-like power of intense sex, or you can choose a love and virtues-based relationship that offers the sweet, satisfying and life-affirming power of intimate sex. But you can't have both at the same time.

If you were to decide that what you really wanted was intensity, then you would want to concentrate on those qualities and behaviors that help boost your adrenaline before engaging in sex. Fear, shame, anger and physical exertion are the four easiest ways to do this. You might go see a scary movie, engage in risky, dangerous or illegal activity, or choose a partner who is likely to hurt, shame or abuse you. Fighting gets the juices flowing too. Exploring the tingle of shame might also offer some interesting options—you could cross-dress, have sex in a public space, or have your partner spank you, for example. You could also try drugs or alcohol to alter the experience and make it more varied and intense.

Oh, there is just one word of caution: If you were to make this choice, no matter what you did, you would have to do something a little more frightening, violent or shameful the next time in order to achieve the same level of intensity. As with other drugs, your body gets used to adrenaline and requires more each time, which means that it is psychologically addictive. Even relatively safe activities eventually evolve into more risky behaviors when their goal is to increase intensity rather than intimacy. But boy, would your sex life be exciting …while it lasted.

Or, instead of the addictive spiral of intensity, you can choose intimacy. Yes, "good old boring intimacy."

Morally upright intimacy.

Spiritually uplifting intimacy.

Sexually stimulating intimacy.

Eternally improving intimacy.

Safe, warm, comforting, satisfying, transformative intimacy.

Intellectually, emotionally and spiritually stimulating intimacy.

Life-enhancing intimacy.

Once Chosen, How Do We Create Intimacy?

Intimacy involves a feeling of knowing and being known; of caring and being cared for, and of physical, mental and spiritual closeness. Intimacy involves sharing—not just sharing physical pleasure, but sharing time, thoughts, dreams, personal goals and spiritual priorities. The pleasure that comes from having sex with someone who knows who you really are—both the good and the bad—and loves you anyway, is more satisfying and long-lasting than the pleasure of intensity.

The foundation of intimacy is trust. Without trust, none of the other aspects of intimacy can be allowed to develop. So let's consider some of the elements of a relationship that will create the trust necessary to foster intimacy.

Honesty is the first. You must know that what a person says is true and that his or her words and actions agree with each other.

On a material level, this may be easy. But on an emotional level, honesty also requires us to know ourselves in order to be true to ourselves. A person who does not know his or her own feelings is incapable of being honest about them. This *inner* honesty is what I wrote about in *4 Tools of Emotional Healing*. Honesty implies a certain level of spiritual and emotional maturity.

Safety is the second essential element for building trust. You must feel physically safe from violence, disease and financial irresponsibility; emotionally safe from betrayal, abuse and abandonment; spiritually safe from self-centeredness, apathy and decadence.

Good character is the third requirement. Becoming intimate is a process in which people share their inner lives. There is a metaphoric "mingling of spirit," so to speak. If a person does not have a good character—if they are not kind, loving, generous, patient, etc.—then what they share will reflect their lack of these qualities and become a source of suffering and even spiritual degradation for their partner. Just as having physical intimacy with a person who is physically unclean can cause disease and even death, so too, emotional and spiritual intimacy with an unhealthy soul can cause spiritual and emotional illness.

Finally, commitment is of paramount importance. Every action has a consequence. Love, sex, intimacy—these all have the potential for long-term physical, emotional and spiritual consequences. It is not safe, it is not honest, and it lacks character to pretend that they only exist "in the moment."

Along with commitment goes perseverance. While it is possible to quickly recognize that you *want* to get to know someone, the process of actually getting to know that person always takes time. When we try to short-circuit the process, we often end up projecting our hopes on someone rather than discovering their reality. We fall in love with the person we want them to be rather than the person they really are.

Taking Time

The simple fact is that everything worth having is worth working for. "Work" involves both time and effort. Playing an instrument, playing a sport, learning to dance, learning to cook, building a house, building a career, learning to listen, learning to care—all of these goals require time and perseverance. Isn't it reasonable, then, to acknowledge that something as important and transformative as love, intimacy and great sex requires (and is worth) the same kind of effort? Think about it.

Spiritual and emotional intimacy develop in stages. We go from strangers to acquaintances, to activities partners, to friends, to close friends, to intimate friends.

"Instant spiritual intimacy" is a fallacy. It is a popular myth because it is very easy to project our fantasies on people rather than wait to see if a person's inner reality matches his or her outer appearance. "We have so much in common … we think so much alike … it was love at first sight."

No matter how much we want these things to be true, we can't know that they are until we spend some time together. If they are true, then the time we spend confirming our initial impressions will be a source of great pleasure and fond memories. But our initial attraction might just as easily be the result of unfinished business. Unless we have the help of an objective outsider, it will take time for us to work out what that unfinished business is. When we do, we will be grateful that we took the time to explore the source of our emotional connection before muddying our perception with sexual attraction.

Physical intimacy also develops in stages, and these stages should follow rather than precede their spiritual counterparts. "Instant physical intimacy" is really a form of exposure. There is an adrenaline rush that comes from laying ourselves out naked on the table (emotionally or physically) that has nothing to do with knowing, caring or moving closer, but a great deal to do with our deep longing to be known and accepted. If we do not establish our emotional safety first, then the vulnerability inherent in exposing this longing will only increase our fear and decrease our true intimacy

Sometimes our desire for great sex has to take a back seat to our larger goals. Sometimes sex has to wait until we deepen our connection with God, develop our virtues and meet some of our social obligations.

Responsible sex always has to wait until we are materially, emotionally and spiritually capable of making a permanent commitment. Waiting shows our partner and the world that we are ready to create a safe environment for nurturing intimacy.

So, are you mature enough to postpone sex until you are physically, emotionally, materially and spiritually ready for it? If not, then you can forget about having great intimate sex because no matter what your age, you won't be bringing to the relationship the qualities that make intimacy possible.

Having Your Cake...

I know what you're thinking—why not have intense sex now and worry about intimate sex somewhere down the road?

Because it doesn't work that way.

Why?

Because you are not a computer, and life is not a game. You can't push a "reset" button and start all over.

Because patterns and habits are hard to change.

Because getting used by different lovers makes you feel jaded and disillusioned.

Because using other people is a sign of irresponsibility and untrustworthiness.

Because you should not put yourself in a situation in which you are defined by your sexual behavior.

Because maintaining intensity requires increasing levels of risk, shame or substance abuse.

Because adrenaline is addictive.

Because risky behavior is addictive.

Because shame is addictive.

Because drugs and alcohol are addictive.

Because sex with people you don't really know only makes you desperate and lonely.

Because the people who are willing to have sex with you without really knowing you are desperate and lonely and not very nurturing.

Because other people will see your actions and begin to believe things about your character that will make it difficult for them to like and trust you.

Because you will observe your own behavior and begin to believe things about your character that will make it difficult for you to like and trust yourself.

Because it is hard to have a healthy relationship with God when you don't like or trust yourself.

Because the person you are looking for is not out there.

Because the person you are looking for is inside of you.

Because making babies is too sacred to do for a cheap thrill.

Because dying of AIDS is too painful to risk.

Because it can waste a lot of precious time.

Because it can waste a lot of precious years.

Because when sex *precedes* commitment, sex *replaces* commitment as the glue that holds a relationship together.

Because lust will blind you to a lover's faults.

Because shame can blind you to a lover's virtues.

Because it will deprive you of the joy of experiencing sex and intimacy for the first time with the person you truly love.

Because it will give you a variety of experiences that no single mate will be able to live up to, and will foster disappointment, jealousy and infidelity.

Because you deserve the best.

Now, while all of the preceding is true, it is also true that nothing in life is black or white. God is forgiving. You will not be damned to hell or addicted to a downward spiral of sexual promiscuity after your first sexual encounter outside of marriage.

But there *are* consequences to our actions. You *can* get pregnant, catch diseases, and start habits after only one sexual experience. Every time we behave in an unhealthy manner, it makes it harder to respond in a healthier way the next time. So why start (or continue) in a direction that will take you somewhere you don't want to go? What would you lose by making the right choice *right now*?

Contrary to popular belief, getting to know someone sexually will *not* increase your chances of making the relationship work. Many studies have indicated that living together, for example, actually *decreases* a couple's odds of having a successful marriage. Many couples remain married for a much shorter time than they managed to live together.

While some would suggest that this means that marriage is bad for a relationship, it really means that *people do not know how to make the transition from a relationship based on intensity to one based on intimacy*. Is it not wiser, then, to begin where you want to end up—with loving, honest, committed, trustworthy, safe intimacy?

What Do We Do in the Meantime?

If intimate sex is the best sex, and it requires time, maturity, commitment, character and the right partner, what do we do in the meantime? Freud would say that we would have to sublimate our sexual urges. I would say that we need to *elevate* them. After all, our desire for sex is a physical expression of our desire for love, and our search for love is a human expression of our longing for God. There are, as we have explored, a myriad ways to express our longing for

God—many of which are very pleasurable.

In its simplest form, sexual intensity is about physical sensations. Physical sensations are very important. They are the tools by which we prove to ourselves that we are physically alive and unique.

It is very important, then, that we not associate delaying sexual interaction with any kind of sensory deprivation. I mean, who would want to delay doing something that makes them feel more alive and unique? If that is how you think of the trade-off between intensity and intimacy, then your subconscious mind will rightfully sabotage your best intentions at every opportunity.

So what is the alternative? Remember, it doesn't work to *stop* doing something. Instead, we need to *replace it* with something better. But replace it with what?

The answer, I believe, is to simply take the next step. Our culture glorifies intense sex, but what we would rather have is *intimate* sex. The next step is to realize that what we are truly longing for is not the sex at all, but the *intimacy*. While we are waiting for the right time and right relationship to have intimate sex, we can enjoy an unlimited number of intimate *friendships*. Not only will they generate their own host of positive spiritual sensations, they will also help us practice the skills we need in order to be successful in the right romantic relationship when we find it.

Disclaimer: when my editor read the preceding page, she wrote in the margins: "Ha! The spiritual sensations of a friendship could never be as much fun as great sex!"

This reminds me of the joke: "Aside from *that* Mrs. Lincoln, how did you enjoy the play?"

In most aspects of our lives, we judge an experience in its totality, not in isolated pieces. One of the signs of addiction is that we focus only on the pleasurable moments of our behavior, trying to isolate them from all of the obvious consequences. If you were to drink a glass of water and discovered dead cockroaches at the bottom of the glass, would you say "that was a great glass of water, except for the last inch?" Or would you say "that was disgusting!" When people talk about how great casual sex is, they are choosing to ignore the feelings of emptiness, shame, fear of disease or pregnancy and guilt that may haunt them for days or years after the few hours of intense physical sensation is a distant memory. Is sex great? Yes...*when* you know you are safe, responsible, loved and committed. Otherwise, not so much.

Intimate friendship may not have the thrilling intensity of three minutes of orgasm, but it really is fun. Getting caught up in stimulating conversations, supporting each other, being of service together, these activities create opportunities to practice virtues that feel wonderful. Meanwhile, the hours, weeks and years of positive interaction they can bring have little or no down side. *Taken as a whole,* healthy friendships are much more fun than loveless sex.

OTHER SENSATIONS
WE MISTAKE FOR LOVE

When we choose intimacy over intensity, we are choosing to base our relationships on true love rather than fleeting sensations.

True love is the recognition of, admiration for and attraction to the attributes of God in another person. There are, however, many emotional sensations that can masquerade as love. I have already talked about fear and shame. Others include need, pity, lust and attachment, along with many subtle variations of love itself.

We have been taught to call these sensations love, and we have learned to respond to them as though they were love. When we learn to identify them accurately, then we can choose to respond to them appropriately. Some of them we will want to avoid. Others we can enjoy, but enjoy for what they really are—interesting messengers, not the foundations for romantic relationships.

An exploration of the many emotions that we mistake for love will increase our awareness of the subtle differences between them. This exercise in emotional semantics will help us recognize the subtle differences between *other* similar emotions. The better we become at discerning the difference between emotions, the richer our emotional and spiritual lives become.

Feeling Loved Is Not the Same as Feeling Love

Feeling loved is the sensation of being acceptable in our entirety. There is a sense of elation that comes from feeling relaxed in this way. We don't have to pretend to be something or someone we are not. Someone has looked in our hearts and seen a piece of God inside.

There is a strength and confidence that comes from having our strengths confirmed and our weaknesses ignored. It is a wonderful feeling, but it has very little relationship to feeling love. It is entirely possible to be loved by someone for whom we feel little love. This is OK. We are not obligated to pretend to see qualities in a person if they are not there.

The problem is when we mistake feeling *loved* for feeling *love*.

It feels so good to feel loved that it is hard to walk away from it. Why would anyone want to burst the euphoria and come down to earth by admitting that they are not attracted to the qualities of the person who sees so much good in them?

Through a combination of guilt and denial, many of us go into relationships with people we are not attracted to, in whom we see very few admirable qualities, simply because we feel loved. Walking away from love is one of the hardest things a human can do. All of the songs, the movies, the books—and certainly, the people we are leaving—are telling us that if one person feels really strongly, then the other person just has to feel the same way or there is something wrong with them.

After the separation, the loss of euphoria combined with the feelings of guilt can cause a real crash in confidence and self-esteem. No wonder many people choose to stay in relationships they are not happy with.

Likewise, it is entirely possible to love people, i.e. see the qualities of God in them, without their being able to see the qualities of God in us. True love does not require reciprocity. Does a painting have to love us in order for us to see the qualities of beauty, harmony and balance in it? Loving someone who is incapable of seeing the good in you is painful, but that doesn't mean there is something wrong with either of you. You may have all of the wonderful qualities they want, but they just can't see them because something in their life has created a veil. Perhaps you remind them of someone who hurt them. Let them have their perceptions. Yours can be different.

When specific people do not appreciate your virtues as you would like them to, rather than getting defensive or depressed, it is helpful to focus less on feeling love and loved, and more on feeling loving and lovable in general.

Feeling Loving and Lovable

While the feelings of *love* and being *loved* are specific to a person or quality, the sensations of feeling loving and lovable are more universal.

Feeling *love* has an object. It is a warm feeling in the heart that increases with the presence or thought of a particular person. It is like a spotlight, illuminating the qualities that we see in a person, and helping us discover even more hidden qualities by its light.

Feeling *loving*, on the other hand, is like sunshine. It makes us want to throw our arms open wide to the world and see the light of God in everyone and everything. As we learn to love more and more individuals, we begin to see their good qualities reflected in the world as a whole. Likewise, as we learn to see the qualities of God in the faces of strangers around us, we become better at loving the individuals in our lives.

When we love, we are looking for the attributes of God in the people and things around us. We feel *lovable* when we look *inside of ourselves* and see just how much we have to offer. Feeling lovable is a lot like feeling loved except, like loving, it is less person-specific. We can feel lovable when we are all alone. Feeling lovable comes with an inner calm, a general awareness that we are acceptable to the universe, no matter what individual people around us may say or do. While loving is a sensation of *radiating* sunlight, when we feel lovable, it feels like we are *basking* in that same light.

When we feel lovable, we are less likely to need to get into relationships in which we are idolized. Having a clear picture of ourselves, we can tell whether a person is seeing the qualities of God we have, or simply the ones they wish we had. We are attracted to people who see us for the children of God that we actually are. Feeling lovable also makes us less needy and less likely to use pity or guilt to attract other's affections.

Worship Is Not Love

Overwhelming love is not love, but worship that is passing for love. There is a big difference between seeing the qualities of God in someone and making them your god. When love crosses the line from admiration to idolization it becomes impossible for mature love to exist. Human love must remain between two humans.

The person being idolized may enjoy feeling loved or resent being isolated on a pedestal, but in either case, it becomes impossible for him or her to admire the qualities of a person who has defined themselves as "less than."

Beware of any "love" that tries to make anyone "special." True love is about recognition of our humanity. Humans are humans. Every human is special. No human is more special than any other. If we use love as a way to feel better than other people, then that love is doomed.

It is one thing to say, "You are special to me" and another to say, "I love you because you are better than everyone else." These are subtle distinctions, but they are distinctions that make the difference between successful relationships and failures. They can also mark the difference between healthy love and dangerous obsession.

Love is about connections between people. Needing to be "better" than your partner or, conversely, needing to find a partner "better" than you creates a separation between the two of you. You can't truly love a person you have separated yourself from. Love between non-equals is possible, for example, as between parents and children or students and teachers. This love acknowledges that there is a separation or distinction in role or capacity. But this kind of love is inappropriate between spouses.

There are two variations of this kind of relationship that are particularly sticky. One is when the person who loves you is the kind who tends to dislike everyone else.

I've had female friends who made a big point of letting me know that I was one of the few men that they could stand to be around. On one hand, this felt like a compliment and was a real ego boost. But it also meant that I was constantly walking the razor's edge. Would the next thing I said be the one to prove that I was just like all of the others? The constant fear of losing my special status meant that my adrenaline was always pumping and I felt energized.

The trade-off for this energy was that I was expected to accept a constant bombardment of negative statements about men in general without taking offense. If I expressed my dismay, it would just prove that I was not special after all. Feeling energized, admired and insulted all at the same time made this particular kind of "love" a deadly poison. This

kind of "I hate everyone except you" approach to relationships is not limited to any one group of people. The critical
and cynical are good at finding people whose self-esteem is
susceptible to this kind of praise.

The other variation involves people who absolutely ooze
love for all of their good friends. Their friends can do nothing wrong and everyone else on the planet pales in com-
parison. Their love is a brilliant heat lamp. The temptation
to do whatever it takes to climb under it can be overwhelming.

I found myself on the edge of such a love one time and
sacrificed one relationship to slide under its influence. I ignored dishonesty, irresponsibility, impropriety and a host
of other flagrant problems so that I could hear this person
tell me how wonderful and talented and creative I was. I
stayed "perfect" for about two weeks. When I made one
mistake, I didn't just fall off of my pedestal; I fell into the
fiery pit. I could suddenly do no right. I was tossed into the
cold and vilified among my friends for the next decade.

But that was OK because, standing outside of the blind-
ing light of "love", I could finally see all of the things I had
been willing to ignore before. My therapist explained that
the "love" I had experienced was never really for me at all. It
was a form of self-love called "Idealizing Narcissism." Having a name for it helped.

I learned the hard way what I should have realized long
before: Feeling loved is not the same as loving, and *loving
the feeling* of feeling loved is one of the most addictive drugs
on the market. Recognize it. Avoid it. Warn your friends.

The ideal, of course, is to both love someone and feel
loved by them. But if we are looking for absolute uncondi-
tional love all of the time, then the only place we can hope
to find it is from God. Every other source of love is human
and subject to change.

Pity Is Not Love

It feels good to care about other people, but there is a difference between loving someone and wanting to take care of them. We care for what we love, but we don't always love what we care for. The act of caring *itself* generates a sensation because it is expressing a virtue. Because it is a positive sensation, it is easy to confuse with love.

A friend of mine knew a boy in high school who was hospitalized after an accident. She didn't know him well, but she went to visit him anyway, just to be kind. She was the only one from her school who did. He was so grateful that she felt obligated to keep coming back. By the time he recovered, they were well on their way to being engaged. It was only after several years of marriage that she looked back and realized that she never *loved* him—was never attracted to his character. She felt sorry for him, and it made her feel good to feel needed. It is called the "Florence Nightingale Syndrome" but it can surface in any relationship in which pity is mistaken for love.

The flip side of mistaking our pity for love is to mistake someone else's pity for *us* as love. That is what my friend's husband did. She was there for him, so he felt loved. He didn't realize that pity and a sense of obligation are not the same as love and respect.

There are a lot of people who make this mistake. They try to get people to love them by constantly complaining about how awful their lives are, or by arranging their lives to be in a constant state of catastrophe. They believe that if people pity them, they will feel obligated to stay around and take care of them. This is the Jewish Mother Syndrome, but you don't have to be Jewish or a mother to use it on people—as my friend discovered.

Need Is Not Love

Need is closely related to pity, but it is more existential in nature. When people do not feel whole or complete or adequate as human beings, they often feel that they *need* someone else to make them complete. Two needy people can find each other and project onto one another the qualities that they think they need to be whole, but these imagined qualities rarely have anything to do with the other person's actual virtues.

Other times, a needy person can latch onto a *savior* or *rescuer* who believes him or herself to possess the right combination of qualities to fix the other person's life. In that case, one person mistakes *need* for love, and the other mistakes being *needed* for love.

Ultimately, we must make a distinction between two people supporting one another as independent human beings, and two people needing each other in order to feel good about themselves. A relationship between two needy people is like two half-people trying to become whole through their partner. It will not survive. A relationship between a needy person and a "rescuer" who believes himself to be a person-and-a-half is based on an impossibility.

If we think in terms of what the other person will do for us or allow us to do, then we *need* them—we don't *love* them. If we think in terms of how much better we will make another person's life and how useful and competent we will feel when we take care of them, then we feel needed, not love.

Lust Is Not Love

Love is not limited to people of the opposite sex, to pretty people, to people of our age or race. Love is an attraction to a person's spiritual qualities. Think about the person you are attracted to. Think about the virtues you have seen this person demonstrate. Think of a specific action that exemplifies this quality… then imagine that same action being done by someone physically unattractive to you. Is that action still charming? Attractive? Inspiring? Appropriate? If not, then it might not be the person's spiritual qualities that you are responding to.

Attachment Is Not Love

If you are having sex with someone, what you are feeling might not be lust, but it might not be love, either. We call sex "making love," but of course sex cannot create love where love does not already exist. What it can do is generate physical attraction and emotional attachments.

This aspect of sex can help keep good relationships from falling apart when they hit temporary challenges. That makes it a useful survival tool for new marriages. It can also hold bad relationships together just long enough to convince people to get married. That makes it one of the biggest reasons why new marriages fail.

To get a feel for the difference between love and attachment, imagine magnets versus Velcro®. Magnets are attracted to each other, even from a distance. When they come together they stick, but you can pull them apart and the attraction remains. They will always return to each other. With Velcro®, there is no attraction, but once the two parts come together (i.e. have sex) then it becomes very difficult to separate them. Yet even in the throes of this attachment, there is this undercurrent that says, "If I ever let go, I'll never see you again." Pull Velcro® apart, and there is no invisible connection working to bring the parts back together.

How many couples have ended their relationships, only to discover that they were never really even friends?

Playing What If?

Perhaps one of the simplest ways to get a sense of what emotion our relationships are based on is to take a few moments and imagine what it would feel like if the relationship were to end, either by the other person's choice or our own.

Relationships based on pity will generate guilt when we contemplate ending them ourselves. If we worry about how guilty we would feel for breaking up with a person, and how bad *they* would feel, then we feel pity and obligation, not love. Likewise, if imagining them breaking up with us gives us a feeling of freedom or relief, then we know that we don't really love them.

On the other hand, if we find ourselves thinking that we cannot live without the other person and that life would be ruined if they were to leave us, then we feel need, not love.

Assuming that a relationship is still fairly new, the thought of saying good-bye to someone we love should generate a sense of deep sadness and loss, but not overwhelming grief, guilt, relief, hopelessness, worthlessness, abandonment, shame or sexual arousal. We should be able to sincerely wish them well and hope that they choose to return, but be able to continue with our own lives if they don't. A relationship can only work if it works for *both* people. A person can't be *your* one-and-only true love unless you are *theirs*.

Avoiding Abusive Relationships

It is impossible to go out looking for a healthy relationship without running the risk of getting sucked into a nightmare. Life is like that. There are excellent resources online for helping you avoid or get out of abusive relationships but they do little good if you don't recognize any of the major warning signs in advance. No one expects to find themselves in an abusive relationship and most people don't even realize that they are in one until some line is crossed. By then, they often feel it is too late to get out.

So the first thing you need to know about abusive relationships is that they can happen to YOU. I know a woman who did her PhD. dissertation on domestic violence in the Hispanic community and only realized afterward that what she had written described her marriage. Abuse crosses all economic, racial, religious, national and gender lines. You are not immune, but you can be inoculated if you pay attention.

Earlier I talked about the difference between need and love, and the difference between being worshipped or made special and true love between equals. One of the most common traps that good, loving people fall into is to become attracted to a wounded soul who has incredible talent, intelligence and potential, but who desperately *needs* someone who is equally special to rescue them from themselves. What starts out as "I need you and can't live without you because you are so loving and special," slowly devolves into the blackmail of, "If you were to leave me, I would do something horrible to myself or someone else." Finally it becomes, "If you threaten to leave me, I will kill you." The heady ego rush of believing that you can save someone who could do great things for the world blinds you to the pathology of the neediness and abuse.

Along this downward spiral, abusers also carefully isolate their victims from family and friends—both physically and emotionally. They will move to isolated areas, create friction with family and alienate friends. Abusers will try to make you feel helplessness and incompetent while at the same time sucking away your financial and emotional resources.

These are just a few of the external warning signs of an abusive relationship, but the most important signs are inside of you. If the thought of leaving generates sensations of either terror or relief instead of loss, then get help right away.

FILLING THE EMPTINESS

In the space between realizing that your old patterns and habits might not work anymore and the development of the skills needed to do it differently, there is a lot of room for panic. That's OK.

It is nice to think about learning how to identify emotions accurately and become attracted to the attributes of God reflected in the hearts of the people around you. Yet I have just listed about a dozen ways of relating to people based on shame, fear, need, pity, attachment, etc. that I claimed are not healthy. If, in reading my descriptions and reviewing your life you come to believe that many, if not most of your relationships are based on something other than love, you may be feeling a bit lost at sea.

So let me offer you three additional observations:

First, no relationship is either all good or all bad. You can need someone and love many of their noble qualities at the same time. You can be sexually attracted and emotionally attracted at the same time. Even the most dysfunctional relationship you have ever had has also had some spark of truth and beauty to it. Everyone reflects the qualities of the Divine, and every relationship is held together, in part, by that spark.

Second and third, it is likely that while you are in transition you will be visited by two uncomfortable sensations: loneliness and anxiety. In this next section, I would like to help you make friends with them.

Overcoming Loneliness

One of the many nice things about developing intimate friendships is that when we have friends, we are less likely to enter into unhealthy romantic relationships simply to avoid feeling lonely. Of all of the sensations that are mistaken for love, perhaps "not lonely" is the most common, and the most empty.

In order to understand loneliness, we need to understand why it is we feel the need to be around people in the first place. For me, there are two reasons. The first is that I need other people to mirror back to me who I am.

If I am creative, or of service to the world and I have no one to share it with, how do I know if I am really creative or not? How do I know I've been of service? God does not generally whisper in my ear or pat me on the back, so I have come to rely on other people to tell me when I am doing well. In a sense, I make other people the mediators of God's approval. I subconsciously try to please God by impressing the people around me.

The second reason I need to be with people is closely related to the first. I have a deep longing to exercise my spiritual capacity; to practice the virtues that God gave me. But most human virtues have to do with how we interact with other souls. I cannot be kind in isolation. It is difficult to be of service while hiding in my room. Generosity, forgiveness, compassion, patience, respect, cooperation, these all involve other people.

So we need human contact, not just to receive positive feedback, but to develop our spiritual potential through the process of giving of ourselves.

Without that human contact, many of us become anxious because we fear we may simply disappear. We fear that without human mediators, we will become invisible to God, and without opportunities to *give* of ourselves we will slowly cease to *be* ourselves.

When we understand the dynamics of our discomfort, we can approach loneliness from three different directions.

First we can forgive ourselves for needing other people. It is not a weakness. It is part of being human.

Second, even though it is natural to seek positive feedback, it is not good to get *all* of our feelings of value from other people. We need to find a higher source for validation—either ourselves or a higher power.

Third, when we *have* to be alone, we can focus on the many virtues that do *not* require the presence of other people. This makes us feel alive and present instead of invisible.

Let me explain these points more fully.

#1: *Forgiving Ourselves*

Our culture values rugged individualism. We are not supposed to need anyone else. We should be brave and confident and not care a hoot what anyone else thinks about us.

Right.

That may sound noble, but in reality it just makes us feel guilty when our natural need for human support surfaces. Remember, *no man is an island.*

One night, as I was struggling with this conflict between my need for human feedback and my desire for independence, I flashed on an image of myself as the filament in a light bulb. Here I was putting out all of this light, but insisting that I didn't need any mirrors to reflect back to me how I was doing. Well, if a light bulb doesn't have anything to bounce its light off of, not only is the light pretty useless, but from the filament's point of view, it can't see any light at all. All it knows is that it is standing in the middle of a vacuum and its heart is on fire.

We all need to see the effect of our efforts, and for most of us, that means we need to see at least some of the people whose lives we touch. We are told not to hide our light under a bushel. Neither should we burn ourselves out in a vacuum.

So it is OK to need to be around people who give us positive feedback about who we are and how we are doing.

#2: *Finding a Higher Source of Validation*

It is good to be able to get at least *some* of your self-esteem from inside yourself. If you depend completely on other people to make you feel good about yourself, then you may find yourself doing things that you don't want to do just to make them happy. You need to know who you are and what you stand for, even when no one else does.

Early in my recovery, I became best friends with a woman who had spent several weeks in a rehabilitation center for codependency. She told me that one of the exercises they had her do was to wear a sign that said, "No male contact." This sounded very difficult to me. I said, "It must have been hard to go a week without touching or hugging a single man." She snorted and said, "You don't understand. I was not allowed *any* contact: no verbal contact, no eye contact, no interaction whatsoever with any male resident or staff."

I remember it clearly. We were driving down a desert highway in New Mexico when she said these words, and as their meaning registered, a panic descended upon me. I felt as though the earth had opened up a bottomless pit in front of me and a howling wind was trying to suck me into it. Just the thought of not having at least one woman look at me every single day felt like soul-death to me. I couldn't imagine surviving it.

So, of course, I knew I had to try it.

It took several weeks for me to build up my courage and arrange my affairs so that I could cut myself off from all human contact for a week, but I did it. No calling friends, no flirting with store clerks or waitresses, no dancing. Just reading, praying and working in my apartment.

I discovered that I really didn't need anyone else to mediate my relationship with God. Even with no one looking at me, I did not disappear or have an anxiety attack. I was who I was, even when I remained by myself for an extended period of time. By seeing myself through my own eyes, I began to get the sense that God *also* saw me through a different set of eyes than the people around me—eyes that were a lot less judgmental than my own or anyone else's. It is good to have self-esteem. But it is even better to know that you have the esteem of the One Who created you.

If you feel the need to constantly surround yourself with people, as I did, then you might find the experience useful.

#3 Finding Virtues We Can Practice Alone

One of the insights that would have helped me get through that week is the realization that part of my need to be around people comes from my need to practice virtues. What I know now is that there are many virtues that do *not* require the direct presence of other people. When I am feeling lonely now, I focus on virtues like creativity, curiosity, knowledge, faith, perseverance, gratitude and many others.

My first therapist gave me an assignment of spending one hour a night doing something creative. Since I'm an artist and writer, you might think this would be something I did all the time anyway. It is strange, though, how, when we are lonely and depressed, we tend to avoid doing the very things that we know make us happy. Creativity is a virtue, and also one of the core attributes of God, so allowing ourselves to express our creativity helps fill the void we feel when our longing for people overshadows our longing for God.

There are also virtues that can be expressed towards people, but at a distance. Research has shown, for example, that writing a letter of gratitude to someone in our past can improve our mood for months, even if we don't deliver it to them face-to-face. This is because practicing a virtue draws us closer to God, even if no one ever knows about it.

Overcoming Anxiety

Loneliness and anxiety often appear together and both can cause a level of desperation in our search for healthy relationships. I'd like to explain the connection and offer some remedies.

When I describe shame, I compare it to the sensation of unexpectedly stepping off of a curb. It is the uncomfortable feeling that you are suddenly falling away from God, virtue and your highest potential. We feel it when we have just done or are contemplating doing something that is not in harmony with our longing for God. If we think about it for a moment, we can name exactly what behavior we are ashamed of.

Anxiety, on the other hand, is the result of a long, slow drift away from God and our spiritual potential. There is no single action or activity that has severed our feeling of connection with God. Rather, we simply wake up in the morning and sense that something is not quite right, that we are heading in the wrong direction; that something bad is going on, but we can't quite put our finger on it.

Psychologists accurately characterize anxiety as a low-grade fear response. What they haven't quite grasped is *what* it is that we are afraid of. Many people feel anxious when there is no rational reason to be afraid. Their material needs are met, their jobs are lucrative, their family is fine, their health is good, and yet they are still anxious.

This is because the fear at the root of anxiety is not about our physical well-being, but our spiritual progress. Anxiety is the subconscious awareness that our longing for God is not being attended to. If we neglect our relationship with God, then we run the risk of drifting farther and farther away from our spiritual reality. We lose contact with the Foundation of our identity and the Source of our virtues. There is nothing in life more terrifying than this. This fear will set the heart trembling and the limbs quaking. I'm not exaggerating. This is the sensation I experienced when I contemplated spending a week alone. I felt anxious because I subconsciously associated being alone with losing my connection with God.

So loneliness is one thing that can cause us to feel disconnected from God, but it is far from the only thing. The fact is, we can be surrounded by people and still have our minds so focused on our material pursuits that our souls feel completely adrift.

While our souls are created with a longing for God, our bodies are born with a need for food, shelter and a host of other material requirements. There is nothing wrong with putting forth a lot of effort to meet those needs. But if that is the *only* thing we focus on as we go through our daily routines, then over time we will feel more and more connected to the material world and less and less connected to our spiritual reality. If we don't focus at least a little bit of attention on our spiritual needs, then even if we do everything *right* in a material sense, we will subconsciously sense that something is wrong.

There are three simple ways to keep ourselves focused on our connection with God. The first is to set aside some time each day to pray and meditate. Consciously turning towards the Transcendent is a good reminder that there is more to life than pursuing our material needs.

The second is to remember to work on developing the virtues that I described in 4 *Tools of Emotional Healing*.

The third way is to continue doing many of the material things you are currently doing, but find a way to put them into a spiritual context. You see, the things we do, in and of themselves, do not draw us closer or farther from our spiritual reality. It is the *motivation* behind what we do that makes the real difference.

If, for example, you pray in the hope of getting rich, then prayer, for you, is a material pursuit. On the other hand, if you go to work each day in order to serve humanity, then your material work becomes a form of worship and is a spiritual pursuit.

When you look at your daily routine in the light of your longing for God, there are some things that you will want to *stop* doing, some things you will want to *start* doing, and a whole lot of things that you will have to *continue* doing. For each of these, try to discover a spiritual benefit or deeper meaning behind it.

If we work to be of service, eat in order to nourish the Human Temple, play in order to connect with our family and friends, read in order to increase our knowledge or deepen our understanding of the human condition, listen to music in order to uplift our hearts, and do all of the other things we do each day as an expression of our love of God, then we will not find ourselves drifting into anxiety. From the outside, our lives might not change much at all, but from the inside, we will be strengthening our connection to the world of the Spirit and letting go of our attachment to the world of dust.

Of course in practice, few people can maintain a spiritual focus every moment of the day. It helps, though, if even once or twice a day you think to yourself, *"Why am I doing this?"* When you can find a *spiritual* answer to that question, you will forge a link between your material actions and your higher spiritual goals. Without this link, life can lose its meaning.

There Are No Deadlines

One of the sources of unnecessary anxiety is our culture's insistence that if you aren't in a romance, then you are drifting farther and farther away from your God-given destiny; that if you don't find your true love by the time you are thirty, then all of your dreams will crumble to dust.

But there are no deadlines for love.

It is much better to spend the next ten years living a life of personal growth and discovery than to get married to the wrong person and then spend years trying to correct the damage you caused.

When I was in my twenties, I was desperate to be married so I could have children before I turned thirty. This desperation led me to get married at 26, only to be divorced at 33. In my thirties, I was desperate to be married again so my wife could have children before we turned forty. I was fortunate to find the *right* person at 38, and my wife had two healthy children *after* she turned forty. Now, at 56, I have adult stepchildren, two teenage kids, a grandchild and enough maturity to deal with all of them. If I live as long as my mother, I have another 30 good years ahead of me— enough to see my kids through college and probably lots of grandchildren.

But what if I hadn't gotten married at 38? What if I got too old to have the biological children that I dreamed of? Think about this: do you really want to get the family and children you planned for, but screw them all up because neither you nor your spouse is emotionally healthy or spiritually suited for each other? If you were forced to choose, wouldn't you rather change your plans and build a different dream?

If your biological clock really does run down, or some other twist of fate means that your life goals get postponed or set aside for twenty or thirty years, it really isn't the end of the world. History is full of people who made their contributions to the world late in life. If you can't have the children you want, you can still adopt or find other ways to contribute love to the planet.

Life is long.

Take your time.

It is important to become the kind of person who can lovingly parent children *before* you look for someone to have sex with.

It is better to spend the last few years of your life with someone you really love than to spend fifty years with someone you pity, need or despise.

How to Find Love

OK, you are working on being attracted to virtues, you are aware of the many sensations that can masquerade as love, you have dealt with loneliness and anxiety, and you are not desperate. You are beginning to like yourself, you are dealing with old family patterns, and you think you are becoming the kind of person that can attract an emotionally healthy person. Now what?

First of all, congratulate yourself. You are already dealing with the most important issues and are far ahead of most people who are desperately looking for love.

Second, appreciate the fact that knowing that real love is a response to a person's virtues will change everything about the way you look for love. Knowing that the sensations that you associate with love are often misleading or inaccurate protects you from wasting time on unhealthy relationships. Nothing else I can tell you will make as big a difference in your future relationships as these two insights.

What I can offer from here on out are secondary observations that apply these two ideas to the process of looking for a life partner.

Signs, Signs, Everywhere a Sign

I will start with this simple caution: *Don't* look for "signs."

If you are a pragmatic person, you probably don't know what I'm talking about, but if you are the kind who is waiting for God to send you your one true love, then you know exactly what I mean.

On my path to finding the "right" woman, I dated one because she had the same vanity plate on her car that I had tried to get. I dated one who had a similar first name and birthday as mine. I dated one who had a similar *last* name as mine. I dated at least four who had had dreams that we were to marry. I dated one who made my knees weak, and another who made my fingers tingle. I dated four Susan's in a row and five variations of Kathy in a row. I dated one woman because we both liked The Beatles. I dated another because we both used the made-up word "fantabulous" *and* had the same Transcendental Meditation mantra. (I was young.) I dated one redhead whose hugs were so soft and warm that I just wanted to melt into her arms—until I realized I was really in love with her down jacket.

In short, I took anything and everything as a sign that God wanted me to try to make a relationship work—that the feelings I was feeling must be true love, not lust or confusion or wishful thinking. Yet none of these relationships worked out.

It wasn't until I stopped looking for signs and started using my head and heart in harmony that I found/created a relationship that worked, and is still working.

Forget "Soul Mates"

One of the reasons why we look for signs is that we believe that there is "one special person" who we are destined to meet and fall in love with. We think that if we miss the signs, then we doom ourselves to loneliness and misery. It was Aristotle who said, *"Love is composed of a single soul inhabiting two bodies."* People have been looking for their other half ever since. Of course, if you review his record, Aristotle was wrong about just about everything—including this.

It takes two whole people to enter into a healthy relationship. If we *think* we have found our soul mate, then we have probably found one of our parents in disguise.

Everyone has the capacity to reflect the attributes of God, so we can love anyone. On a planet with almost seven billion people, the search for the "right one" is hopeless. Just trying will make us anxious and desperate. But when we realize that that same seven billion includes *millions* that would be perfectly compatible if we put forth the effort, then we can relax and enjoy the search.

Get an Outside Perspective

I encourage you to do the one thing that people who *think* they are in love are loath to do: get a third (fourth and fifth) opinion. For this, I encourage you to consider a professional therapist, as well as parents, siblings and trustworthy friends.

By "getting a person's opinion" I don't mean you should ambush them with the news that you are in love and ask for their blessing. I mean you should ask someone you respect to share their opinion about your partner's character; what they think the strengths and weaknesses of the person (and a potential relationship) might be. If they say good things, ask for examples. If they say bad things, ask for examples. If they say nothing … well, you know what that means.

To be honest, I did not ask my friends' opinions. Instead I made an agreement with my therapist. I had been dating women non-stop for four years. At the end of my next-to-last relationship, my therapist asked me if I might have been able to predict the outcome earlier.

I had to admit that I was fully aware of all of the reasons why the relationship was doomed even before I entered it, yet the "signs" and my own wishful thinking had led me into it anyway.

So my therapist and I made a deal: I would not consider another woman romantically unless I could describe her to my therapist and answer probing questions about her *before* I got romantically involved.

As it turned out, I did not need my therapist's brilliant insights and probing questions to figure out that the next several women I thought about dating were not a good idea. All I had to do was imagine myself describing them to my therapist. I already knew exactly what the fatal flaws in the relationships were before I even started them.

After having gone from one relationship to another for four years, it was six months before I dated again. When I finally brought a name to my therapist, I didn't even really need her approval (though I got it). I knew that this person was different from the rest because I had entered into the friendship differently. This was the woman I decided to marry, and we are still together eighteen years later.

Make Lists

If you don't know what you want, you will waste a lot of time and heartache chasing something else. When I encourage you to make a list, I don't mean that you should decide what your ideal partner will look like or any of the incidentals. Your list should include your bottom-line requirements. It is OK to have a secondary list of "wouldn't it be nice if…" but if you go for that and ignore your non-negotiables, you will be doing yourself and your relationships a disservice.

For me, my list had four lifestyle requirements and four values requirements, but yours may not be the same. That is for you to decide, though I hope that this book has given you some valuable insights into what you want to spend your life with.

My list was:

Willing to join my religion.
Willing and able to have children.
Willing to participate in couple's therapy.
Non-smoker.
Both intelligent and sweet.
Honest.
Responsible with money.
Single, female.

At the time, I had not developed my thoughts on honesty, forgiveness, compassion and faith, but I suspect my understanding of "sweet" included elements of compassion and forgiveness. "Join my religion" certainly included an openness to faith, so in many ways my old list included the same qualities I would look for today.

Though there are only eight things on this list, the "join my religion" requirement quickly eliminated almost everyone on the planet. My fear that there would be no one in the world who both met my minimum requirements and would be willing to commit to me drove me to compromise on one or more of these requirements in relationship after relationship.

As a result, I wasted years of time and lost a great deal of integrity by pursuing inappropriate and ill-fated relationships. I can't guarantee you that sticking to your minimum requirements will magically make your perfect match appear, but I *can* guarantee you that *pretending* to be willing to compromise (just so you won't be alone) will *not* bring you what you want. It will anger those you have misled and call into question your integrity.

The last few pages may not seem like much in terms of guidance for finding someone to spend your life with, but combined with the insights of the rest of the book and the previous two in this series, it is much more than most of us ever dreamed of having when we set out to find true love. Remember to focus on virtues, and continue to question the hidden meaning of the emotional sensations you experience, and you will figure out anything else you need to know.

FROM LOVE TO COMMITMENT

For many years, my beliefs about love were entangled with my thoughts on marriage. I tried to keep myself from loving anyone I couldn't marry. I received a great gift when I fell in love with a married woman. I realized then that if I could love a person I *couldn't* marry, then I could also allow myself to love people I didn't *want* to marry.

I now know that love and marriage are completely different things. Love is like going to school. Marriage is like choosing a career. When you go to school, you can study anything that interests you—science, art, literature, history—you can find something to love in any subject.

That is how love should be. Everyone you meet has an interesting story and reflects a unique constellation of virtues. If you look hard enough, you can find something about them to love.

But marriage is like choosing a career. You balance what you enjoy against what helps you achieve your long-term life goals. You should never choose a career that you hate, but that doesn't mean that you will choose the career that you find the most stimulating. Some relationships are like French Poetry. They may express virtues that you enjoy experiencing, but that doesn't mean you can build a life around them.

As in choosing a career, it is not enough to know what you love. You also have to know what you want out of life. Do you want children? Do you need financial security? What country do you want to live in? Are you a city or country person? Do you smoke? These goals represent other virtues that you love. Some of these goals are non-negotiable and will eliminate a large number of perfectly wonderful people from your list of potential mates. That is okay. It is not a crime to balance your immediate passions with your long-term loves.

If you truly understand the difference between love, sex and marriage, then you can continue to love and enjoy a wide range of people after you commit yourself to be faithful to and build a life with your marriage partner. After all, we all have hobbies outside of our careers. You wouldn't, however, choose a hobby that would destroy your career.

A surgeon doesn't take up boxing as a hobby. A married person doesn't hang out with sex addicts. Trust is as easily broken as hands.

Building a Healthy Relationship

Ultimately, the surest way to avoid temptation and remain faithful is to keep your current relationship as strong, honest and secure as possible.

While this is not a marriage manual, I do have a couple of insights that you might find helpful.

The first is to simply *be happy with the person you are with*. Don't try to make them happy. Don't make them try to make you happy. Being happy with yourself is a life-long process, but being happy with the people around you is a here-and-now proposition. We can do it if we choose to.

While learning to be happy may be a lifelong process, learning to be happy with the person we are married to is much easier. We have to live with our own inner demons, but we only have to live with our spouses *outer* demons. That's a lot less work.

Being happy with our spouses is also much easier than trying to make *them* happy with *us*. That is the codependent's misguided path to happiness. Just as I am responsible for my own happiness, I cannot *make* anyone else happy. What I can do is focus on all of the positive things about my spouse and choose to be happy about them.

In *The Secret of Emotions*, I compared the sensations of love to the scent of a rose. I said that the scent of love does not go away, but our awareness of it does. If we make a conscious effort to remind ourselves of the virtues that our partner brings to the relationship, then we will enjoy being around them. They may not do what we want them to do, or be the person we thought they would be when we married them, but they are still children of God, struggling just as we are to learn how to reflect the Divine.

One step in the process of becoming happy with the one you are with may involve resigning yourself to the simple fact that you may *never* receive from them what you hoped to get. The fact is, *whatever* it is you want, it isn't anyone else's job to give it to you. We long for God, yet we look to other humans to give us things that symbolize the things that only God possesses.

Here's the distinction you need to be able to make: There is a difference between a spouse who cannot or will not give you what you need, and a spouse who actively tries to take from you what you try to generate yourself. If a spouse is abusive; if they rob you of your dignity, self-esteem, security and identity; if their untrustworthiness undermines your well-being, then you need to go elsewhere. These are the abusive relationships that I mentioned earlier. There are online checklists you can find to help you identify these relationships, both before and after you get caught in one.

But…if they are unable to give you *more* of these things than you can generate for yourself, then they are simply human. Look to God for these things, and much, much more, and be happy with your spouse for being willing to walk the path towards God with you. That's really all that any of us can ask from another person.

The people who live in our fantasies are just that: fantasies. Even if we put a name and face and body to the fantasy, until we live with them day in and day out, we can't know if they would be any more able to meet our needs than the one we are with. Until we accept and love and support our current spouses on their path towards God, we can't know the heights that our present relationships might achieve.

Being Sexually Content

Often, the problem we *think* we have with our spouse is really a problem caused by our inability to make the transition from a relationship based on intensity to one based on intimacy.

As I've explained, a relationship based on love and trust and security generates a *completely different range of sensations* than one based on intensity. Many of us *start* our relationships with a sex-life based on intensity. Sex outside of marriage, though socially acceptable for many people, still carries the excitement, titillation and shame aspects of the forbidden fruit. Once a relationship is sanctioned by the church and state, much of that extra energy starts to wear off. If we expect sex to maintain that intense edge after marriage, then we begin to think something is wrong—with us, with our partner, or with our marriage. If it doesn't wear off after marriage, it often does after a first child is born and couples start seeing each other as parents rather than sex partners.

If we have a long history of sexual activity based on intensity, how do we change our habits and adjust our expectations?

The unfortunate answer is that once a set of habits has formed, it can take an incredible amount of conscious effort to re-educate our unconscious responses.

While I firmly believe that we can re-train both our physical and our spiritual attractions, re-training our spiritual attractions is certainly the easier of the two. If we are young and our partner is understanding, then it can be just one more process of discovery that can be explored in the years ahead. If we are old and our expectations, habits and preferences are deeply ingrained, then it might be too much to ask of our partners to struggle through our process of transformation.

If one partner is drawn to excitement and shame, while the other only responds to security and affection, then there may be no happy compromise between these two needs. Or, if one is drawn to shame and the other is repelled by it, then even communication between the two may be impossible.

Most often, however, both partners were originally attracted to the forbidden fruit of passionate sex, and now that the relationship is sanctioned by God and consummated with children, there is no fear, shame or excitement left to inspire passion.

In this case, you have to decide which is worse: having a sexually tepid marriage, or having a marriage that is subconsciously conspiring to generate fear and shame in order to recapture the sexual tension of the pre-marital pseudo-romantic period.

If the thought of a tepid sexual relationship with your partner sends you into the kind of bottomless pit of panic that the thought of being alone gave me, then you may need to think about what that means for you. If you and your partner are both young, with only a few years of patterns to break, then reorienting your sex life around love and intimacy may be very easy. If you are older, with lots of patterns, expectations and habits, then it might take a lot of effort to change. How many hours, days or years of your life do you want to devote to this? If your partner is not as driven as you are to develop new ways of interacting, then it might be impossible to restart your sexual relationship on a more spiritual foundation. That doesn't mean that you can't build a more intimate spiritual relationship. It just might never be as sexually satisfying as you fantasize.

Building Spiritual Relationships

Ultimately, our sexual relationship with our spouse is only a tiny sliver of our over-all relationship. It is only as important as we make it.

Our spiritual relationship, on the other hand, can support us in our individual striving after God, and can last on into the next world. If we apply the virtues of honesty, forgiveness, compassion and faith to our most important human relationship, then it can't help but improve over time. As our primary relationship improves, our temptations, obsessions, addictions and shame will become less of a distraction on our path towards God.

Avoiding Globalizing

When we love someone, we are not just attached to them sexually. We are spiritually attracted to a whole host of interconnected virtues. One of the benefits of seeing our partners as this constellation of positive qualities is that it helps us to avoid globalizing.

I mentioned globalizing in the section on forgiveness in book two when I said that we should not label an entire person based on one negative quality or action. The reverse is also true. When we fall in love with a person, we tend to globalize their positive qualities, which can then be used to mask a person's flaws.

There is an expectation in our culture that if you are going to love someone, you must love them *warts and all*. But that is not really healthy. We don't need to pretend to *love* a person's faults in order to *accept* their faults as a part of who they are. Trying to love *all* of a person is the kind of *all or nothing thinking* that led to perfectionism when we applied it to ourselves. When we try to use the same kind of black-and-white thinking in our relationships, it causes us to see our partners as either wonderful and loving, or the source of all of our problems.

If, instead, we see people as a constellation of virtues—some of which are well-developed and some of which are weak—then we can realistically adjust our response to each character trait individually.

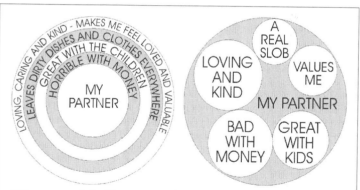

When we globalize, we only see one quality at a time. We alternate between seeing only good and only bad. When we see people as a constellation of virtues, we see all of their qualities at once, and relate to them as a whole person with strengths and weaknesses.

How to Remain Faithful

This section is about dealing with temptation. While many of the specific issues addressed will focus on sexuality, relationships and unhealthy attractions, the principles involved in avoiding temptation can be applied to almost any behavior that we have difficulty controlling. From infidelity and pornography to overeating and smoking, there are many actions we feel compelled to engage in, even though we know they are not spiritually, emotionally or physically healthy.

The best way to deal with temptation, of course, is to avoid it. In *The Secret of Emotions*, I shared this parody of our compulsive behaviors:

> *Find a cookie.*
> *Tell yourself that eating the cookie is a bad idea.*
> *Eat the cookie anyway.*
> *Regret eating the cookie.*
> *Deal with guilt by looking for more cookies.*

The first step is always finding a cookie. If you don't go looking for a cookie, you are much less likely to be tempted by it. In other words, avoid people, places and things that send your mind or your body in a direction that you know is unhealthy for you. For example, if you hope to find or maintain a healthy, committed relationship, then avoid sex addicts, bars, massage therapists, adult bookstores and movie theaters, swimming pools, co-ed fitness clubs, web-surfing alone at night and anything or anyone that gets your hormones pumping.

Sometimes, though, the world throws cookies in our laps. Seriously. Unless we lock ourselves in a tower with no contact with the outside world, we *will* face temptation. So what do we do then?

For most people, the standard response is to "tell yourself not to eat the cookie." That is, throw shame and guilt at ourselves as a punishment for even *thinking* about eating the cookie.

As I explained before, this is counter-productive. First of all, if we are going to punish ourselves *before we even take a bite*, then we might as well go ahead and do what we feel guilty for. Second, the unhealthy action is usually one that generates a sensation strong enough to temporarily turn off the guilt and shame. So guilt and shame actually push us towards the behaviors they are warning us about.

Our first step, then, is to remind ourselves that it is normal to want the cookie. *Of course* we want a cookie. We are human. This helps defuse the shame.

After this, there are several alternative responses. We can distract ourselves, devise a long-term reward for refusing temptation, devise a short-term reward or consequence, or explore the deeper longing.

Distraction is certainly the easiest, but like most alternatives, it requires forethought. Often temptation springs out of nowhere and hijacks our rational minds with unexpected and intense sensations. Thrown into such a situation, it is difficult to focus on anything except the tempting opportunity in front of us. Whether we encounter it by walking past a bakery or walking past an adult video store, having a list of alternative activities or points of focus can be a real life-saver.

These could include:

Saying a prayer or affirmation.
Going to a 12-step meeting or calling a sponsor.
Calling a close friend to talk.
Working on a creative project.
Going for a walk or jog.
Taking a shower.
Getting a haircut.
Downloading a new song to listen to.
Singing a song to yourself.
Reading a book.
Thinking about your children or other loved ones.
Counting backwards from 100.

This last one might seem way too short to be of any use, but the fact is that most sensations only last a few minutes if we don't feed them with shame or fantasy. If we can get ourselves around the metaphoric corner, then we are half-way home.

Long-term rewards work for some people. The promise of going to heaven, finishing school and starting a career, having a happy and healthy family—these have successfully motivated many people to walk away from temptation and make healthy choices.

If those motivations worked for you and me, however, we probably wouldn't have lived the lives we have. That is why researchers in the science of self-control recommend coming up with short-term rewards and punishments (*other* than guilt and shame) to help us overcome our tendency to settle for immediate gratification. It is also why AA has a coin to celebrate 24 hours of sobriety as well as one week, one-month and one-year coins.

Depending on the temptation you are trying to escape, coming up with a way to reward yourself after one day, one week or one month of success is a great way to change your focus when temptation knocks.

Gentle punishments can also help pull us away from actions that are unhealthy—but be careful that your feelings of unworthiness don't cause you to slip up so that you can dish out the punishment you already think you deserve. Instead, be creative.

For example, I heard a story about two sisters. One smoked and the other didn't. The one who didn't vowed to donate $1,000 to the Ku Klux Klan if the other sister ever smoked another cigarette. The sister quit smoking cold-turkey rather than allow money to be given to an organization she despised.

You might try something a little less extreme, like giving $50 to a cause you dislike, or scrubbing your toilet, or doubling the number of 12-step meetings you go to, or confessing your slip to your sponsor or therapist.

Ultimately, though, I believe that staring temptation in the face and asking it to explain itself to us may be the best way to get it to back down. When we respond to temptation with, "Oh, I'm such a horrible person, I'm so guilty, I'm so ashamed," we are really being self-indulgent. We are wallowing in our own low self-esteem instead of looking at our actions objectively and considering how they affect the world around us.

88

Dealing with Inappropriate Attractions

My friend Phyllis Peterson, author of *Remaining Faithful* and *Assisting the Traumatized Soul*, asked me to address a very concrete challenge that many of us face. She asked:

> *One facet of the challenge we face is learning to work together, associate together without sexuality becoming our focus. How do we act with maturity? How do we overcome an adolescent response to someone who may take our breath away?*

My answer is that we *pay attention*. We look our uncomfortable sensations in the eye and try to name them accurately. We shine a light on every response that appears to draw us away from our highest good.

We remember that sensations are messengers, and that once the message has been accurately received, the sensation often evaporates. We keep no secrets. And in the meantime, we take appropriate action to protect ourselves and others from rash and foolish actions.

That doesn't sound like very concrete advice, so let me give you an example from my own life.

I was attending a workshop on the Authenticity Project. This is a very intense workshop that deals with the most profound levels of human interaction. The conversations between breaks were refreshing and stimulating.

There was one young lady whose comments were particularly stimulating. She was stunningly beautiful, had a French accent and was so full of life and energy that she was a joy to talk to. I was immediately drawn to her and joined her circle of conversation every chance I got. The problem was that every time I was near her, my heart would race and my whole body would go on high alert. It was embarrassing. I was a married man, and she was twenty years younger than I was.

I went to bed that night with my mind in an uproar. Why was my body reacting this way? Was I really that lecherous that I couldn't talk to a young woman without getting aroused?

If I hadn't already been aware of the difference between love and lust, I could have easily convinced myself that I was in love and that I should leave my wife and run off with this woman. Fortunately, I knew that sensations don't always mean what we think they do.

So I sat myself down and had a little conversation with myself. Did I want to have sex with this young woman? I took a serious look around my heart and concluded that I really didn't.

This reaction wasn't about desire at all. But if the sensation wasn't about sex, then it was probably that *other* sensation—shame. But why would I feel shame if I weren't already thinking about having sex with her? What was I ashamed of? Was I afraid I was going to be unfaithful to my wife? No. Did I enjoy talking with her? Yes. Was she intelligent? Yes. Was I going out of my way to talk with her? Yes. But if she was intelligent and fun to talk with, why shouldn't I go out of my way to do so?

Because it looked bad.

Oh. I wasn't embarrassed because I wanted to have sex with her. I was embarrassed because I was afraid that she would *think* that I wanted to have sex with her. I was afraid of looking like a dirty old man, when all I wanted to do was have an intelligent conversation with someone who just happened to be young and beautiful.

Some of you are probably thinking, "*Who does this guy think he's fooling?*

But I know that this was the source of my feelings because the next morning, I did the unthinkable. I told her.

I went up to her and said, "I need to tell you that I've been feeling uncomfortable around you because you are so young and beautiful, I was afraid that you would think that I was trying to flirt with you when I'm not. I just really enjoy talking with you."

She said, "Oh, don't worry. I didn't think that at all. I enjoy talking with you, too."

And suddenly, all of those strange sensations evaporated. She became a normal human being. We spoke many times over the course of the weekend, and that was the end of that. No romance. No riding off into the sunset. No clandestine rendezvous, and no more shame.

Knowing What Love Doesn't *Feel Like*

I was fortunate that I could tell that what I was feeling was *not* love. That allowed me to go pounding on internal doors until I figured out what the feeling really was.

Knowing what it *isn't* is a valuable first step. If your heart is going pitter-patter, or your knees get weak, or your fingers tingle, or any of the dozens of Hollywood stereotypical sensations hit you over the head, then you can rest assured that what you are feeling is *not* love. That means that you can safely explore all of the other options without getting distracted.

If it's not love, you don't have to worry about leaving your spouse and destroying your marriage. If it's not love, then sex is clearly inappropriate. If it's not love, then it's not your one-and-only chance at happiness. If it's not love, then you don't have to *do* anything about it until such time as you figure out what it *is*.

If it's not love, you can honestly describe it as a *strange* or *uncomfortable* physical sensation. If you describe it to yourself in this way, it may help you name it.

You can also tell your spouse, *"I experience a strange and uncomfortable sensation when I'm near that person. Do they cause you to react in any way?"* This is so much better than, "I think I'm in love with the new person I just met. May I run off with them, please?"

Other possible causes for the sensations we feel around attractive people can include:

Fear that we will be rejected by them if we approach them in friendship.

Fear that they will accept us at first, then abandon us.

Fear that they will treat us the way the family member they remind us of would.

Embarrassment because they are prettier, richer, taller, stronger, younger, more talented, etc., than we are.

Fear that they will be able to identify some fatal flaw in our lives.

Embarrassment that they appear to be inappropriately attracted to us.

Fear of authority figures.

Subconscious recognition of the fact that they are predatory, abusive, sex addicts, dishonest or violent.

Remember, our emotions tell us about our spiritual environment by sending us signals—both physical and spiritual. If you are experiencing Unidentified Feeling Obsessions (UFO's), then there is probably something going on spiritually that you need to figure out. When you do, it will become a CSI—a Clear Spiritual Insight, and the sensation will fade.

Can Men and Women be Friends?

Absolutely.

Can every man stay friends with every woman? No.

This is a question that requires a supreme amount of self-knowledge, perception and sensitivity.

In the future, I think this will be much easier, but right now, our culture is so focused on sex that it is difficult for two single people to maintain friendships, and those between a married and a single person can be difficult.

What I have found helpful is to remind myself that my soul and my body function in two completely different ways. As long as I don't let my soul be confused by what my body tells me, then I'm safe.

To be specific: In any interaction between a healthy male and a healthy female, there will come a moment in which their bodies will become aware of their sexual reality. It might be at first sight, it might be months into the friendship.

At that point, the soul has a choice. It can say, "Oh, my God, I'm sexually attracted to this person. What will I do? What does this mean? Is this the end of our friendship?"

Or, the soul can say, "Hmm. Interesting. My body just noticed the obvious. That is what the body is supposed to do. But it doesn't mean anything. Physical attraction is like a cloud in the sky. If you don't seed it with fantasy, it will simply blow over."

If you try to ignore the attraction, as I've said before, you just give it the power of secrecy and shame. If you look it straight in the eye and say, "Thank you for reminding me that I am alive, but I'm not interested in moving in that direction," then the attraction will usually kiss you on the cheek and walk away.

I have many, many female friends, including some of my previous girlfriends. I work with women, hang out with women, e-mail women, even dance with women. I stay aware of which ones I might be tempted by and avoid dangerous situations. I tell my wife about everyone I correspond with, and introduce her to as many of my female friends as I can.

She tells me which women she considers dangerous and I agree to not spend time alone with them.

My wife, in turn, has male friends.

Dealing with Compulsive Behaviors

What do we do if we find ourselves sexually aroused by shoes, cross-dressing, children, nuns, dolls, exhibitionism or anything or anyone that our religion or moral compass considers inappropriate?

By now, I don't need to tell you that much of what our culture describes as attraction and the symptoms of love is actually our body's response to intense shame or fear.

You already *know* that true spiritual attraction is not the same thing as fear or shame. So when fear or shame causes our bodies to react inappropriately, what do we do? Even though we may not be able to change what we fear, or escape our subconscious shame triggers, we *can* change how we respond to them.

We can choose to walk *away* from these sensations rather than running *towards* them. If we find a *different* sensation to call attraction—a *warm and loving* sensation, then we can change who it is that we choose to become lovingly intimate with.

In our culture, we call fear love, and then insist that we can't change who we love.

But if that were true, then women who are "attracted" to abusive men would be doomed to only be with abusive men. That is crazy. A woman becomes aroused around an abusive man because she subconsciously senses his capacity for violence, and it frightens her. It is *fear* arousal, not *love* arousal that she feels.

When we understand the true source of the sensations that we define as attraction, we can change our definitions. We can call spiritual attraction *love*, and shame-based attraction *arousal, lust, fear, shame* or *desire*. When we name them accurately, it is easier to choose between them.

We Are Not Defined by Our Desires

If I defined myself by my lusts, I would not be defined as a very spiritual being. During the years between my divorce and my second marriage, I came to realize that my desire for every single woman that I had ever thought I was in love with was based on some deeply-seated dysfunction. Because my older sister was mentally ill and sexually abused, and my mother was afraid of men, the women I was physically and emotionally attracted to were, without exception, some combination of:

Mentally ill.
Sexually abused as children.
Angry or fearful of men.

Because my father left my mother with a house full of children when I was just developing my identity, I also found myself desiring women who were considering divorce, or had just gotten divorced, and had children at home under the age of seven. I could literally sit in a bar and point to women from across the room and tell you what their dysfunction was, based on my physical response to them. The soul is amazingly perceptive.

So, if I were to define myself by my "natural" desires, then I could call myself a:

Schizosexual.

Abusexual.

FearSexual.

And/or Divorsexual.

If this sounds like an absurd way to identify oneself, then you can see the fallacy in someone identifying themselves primarily by their emotional or physical desires. We are all humans, and we each happen to respond physiologically to different types of stimuli. Big deal.

In *The Secret of Emotions*, I said that being able to accurately name and define our emotions gives us a certain amount of power over them. This principle applies to *us* as well. Defining ourselves by our emotional desires, especially if those desires are fear- or shame-based, gives those desires an excessive amount of control over our lives.

When we see ourselves as spiritual souls on a path to God, then it becomes obvious that *we* have the capacity to be in control of our attractions and our desires, rather than the other way around.

If I were to assume that my attractions are set at birth and are unchangeable, then I would be foolish to try to fall in love with or marry someone who is not crazy, abused, afraid and divorced.

If, however, spiritual attractions and physical desires are both the result of life experiences and are subject to transformation, then I can consciously *choose* the kind of person I want to marry and raise a family with. I can then train myself to recognize and become attracted to this kind of person.

I can also make a conscious distinction between spiritual attraction and shame-based physical desire, and choose to prioritize the sensations of love over the sensations of shame. After all, which is more important—the buzz my body experiences when a person generates a jolt of adrenaline in my presence, or the warm feeling I get when a person demonstrates kindness and responsibility in my presence?

I can't stop myself from reacting to the presence of people who remind me of my past, but I can stop calling that reaction attraction. I can name the sensations I feel *fear, shame, pity,* or simply *confusion,* and behave accordingly. I can also learn to recognize true attraction to the spiritual qualities of the people I meet, and respond appropriately to them.

If I can do it, so can a person who is aroused by abusers, or alcoholics, or children, or high-heeled shoes, or cross-dressing, or pornography, or any partner that is not spiritually and emotionally healthy.

Don't Feed the Shame

Instead of telling ourselves how horrible we are for doing something, we could be asking ourselves why in the world we would want to do it in the first place.

I've talked a lot about how different experiences generate sensations and how easy it is to misinterpret those sensations. What I haven't addressed is just how *unsatisfying* those sensations really are. After all, they are generally *substitute* sensations—ones generated by the third-cousin once-removed of the spiritual quality we are really seeking.

When we can identify the longing for God that is hidden in the experience, we begin to see the chasm between what we are doing and what we really want and need. Suddenly the temptation is not so tempting. It becomes a farce, a charade, a ludicrous pastime that wastes the precious hours of our day that could be spent doing something real and true and life-affirming.

Nowhere is this gap more obvious than in the temptation of pornography.

Pornography

Let me start by shocking some and angering others in saying that pornography (assuming it involves consenting adults), is not that big of a deal. Many married couples watch pornography together. If you don't have one partner hiding, sneaking or lying to the other, it doesn't do much harm.

Of course, it is also not all that much fun anymore. If you take away the guilt, the shame and the adolescent titillation, pornography is generally about as interesting as watching two people churning butter. The music is awful, the acting is worse, the plots are absurd, and the production quality looks like it was filmed in someone's garage. Oh, right—they usually are.

So if pornography is so poorly made, why do people find it so exciting? Here is what a pornography addict wrote to me once:

In many ways I feel so alive when watching pornography, and yet, I am so .... sexually charged. I am afraid I will not stop at just pornography or sexual chatting online......

This was my answer to him (some of which you already know by now):

Our souls have experiences that generate physical sensations. These sensations are signals, or messages from our souls to our bodies. Our minds then try to interpret what those sensations mean. It is our interpretations, not the sensations themselves, that guide our actions. If we interpret wrong, then we will respond incorrectly to the messages we are receiving.

If I were to throw you overboard into icy arctic water, you would suddenly feel very much "alive." Every cell in your body would react in an attempt to KEEP you alive as you recognized the imminent threat of death. The same systems that would respond slightly if you stepped outside without a jacket in winter would go into high alert to warn you that something was wrong.

You are not feeling "alive" and "sexually charged." You are feeling *shame*.

Your soul is warning you that your relationship to your wife and family may be at risk. Shame is a signal that we have just done, or are about to do, something imperfect. It reminds us that we are human and can make mistakes.

It is a helpful signal. When we feel a little bit of shame, we flush and feel a slight tingle in our face and hands. When we are about to do something that can cause irreparable harm to our spiritual lives, then the signal gets louder. Sometimes a LOT louder. *So* loud that it becomes a wake-up call.

But when we feel asleep, or even dead, sometimes that warning signal—the tingling in our arms and legs, the racing of our hearts, the hyper-alertness of our senses—feels more like a pleasant gift than a warning.

When this happens, the sensations that were designed to make us STOP, TURN AROUND, GO BACK, THINK IT OVER are interpreted as: "LOVE, LIFE & EXCITEMENT – THIS WAY!!"

Unfortunately, just like the sensations of being thrown into ice water, if you revel in them, they will lead to your (spiritual) death. They will not bring you love. They will not give you a better life. They will only lead to the kind of excitement that leads to more shame. Take the warning, and change direction.

At the same time, recognize the fact that this wake-up call only felt good because you were already feeling asleep and dead. Start there. Find people and activities that make you feel awake and alive, instead of shame. You will be able to tell the difference both in the way your body feels and in your ability to share the details of them with your wife and family.

No spouse can meet all of a person's mental, physical, social and spiritual needs, but they can take pleasure in hearing the stories of how they were legitimately met elsewhere. Service organizations, clubs, work, community activities, writing, reading, prayer, singing, exercise, hobbies, gardening—there are many ways to feel spiritually alive.

* * *

What we are looking for is love, affection, connection, a sense of belonging and a belief in our own worthiness. But the physical sensation associated with self-stimulation leaves us feeling *less* loved, *less* connected and *less* worthy of affection.

So the first step in letting go of pornography is to look at it in the light of day and admit that it isn't helping us feel what we *want* to feel. It is only making us feel *something. Something* is better than *nothing*, but not by much.

Next, let go of the shame. It only feeds the addiction. Pornography is simply the pure distillation of what our sex-obsessed culture throws at us every single day. Yikes! The cover of that magazine has a nearly-naked woman on it! Yikes! The woman who walked by was wearing her underwear on the outside. Yikes! That thirteen-year-old is wearing a "foxy lady" tank top! Yikes! Aunt Fritzi has awfully big breasts!

Getting embarrassed by our response to the images we are bombarded with and the people we are surrounded by only gives them more power. If we feel guilty or embarrassed for noticing the obvious, we will try to *fight* the obvious, which will just keep us focused on it that much longer.

It helps to realize that *all* men are hard-wired to have a hard response to visual images of women, especially young, beautiful women. If the hip-to-waist ratio is right, a healthy adult male will respond instinctively.

Visual stimulation does not affect women in the same way, which makes it difficult for them to understand its allure for men. Women don't understand that, for a man, walking down a crowded street in springtime is like walking past rows of bakeries and chocolate shops. The sight of attractive women is just as stimulating as the scent of donuts and chocolate. It cannot be controlled any more than we can stop our mouths from salivating at the scent of a croissant.

Women, of course, are not exempt from the lures of pornography, they just call it by a different name. Just as the internet has revolutionized the availability of visual sexual images for men, the e-book revolution has made erotic romance the fastest growing category of downloadable books. Women can become just as aroused by the written descriptions of sex as men are by pictures, and those written descriptions have just as much potential to involve shame, violence and fetishes as a video. (Witness the runaway sales and the social acceptability of *Fifty Shades of Gray.*) The difference is that a woman can read an erotic e-book in a crowded room and no one will even notice.

It is also easier to ambush men with visual images than to trick women into reading erotic literature, so men find themselves being constantly tempted.

Men are also hard-wired to get an erection several times a day for no discernable reason whatsoever. It doesn't mean we are horny. It means we are healthy.

When we expect men to be able to control their passing thoughts *and their autonomic nervous systems*, we set them up for continual failure and shame. What we *can* control is how we respond to the ways our bodies react.

When we experience a flash of arousal, it is tempting to focus our attention on it. After all, it feels *good* to have your groin tingle for a moment. Since these sensations tend to be fleeting, it is tempting to do something to try to prolong them, like grab a magazine or pop open a web site.

If, however, we let the thought or the sensation have its moment and then let it go without focusing on it or fighting it, then it will fade. If we consciously choose to shift our focus *away* from the sensation, then pornography will have less allure. We can't stop thoughts from coming to us, but we can keep them from hanging around and affecting our behavior.

This is equally true of thoughts we might consider disturbing or inappropriate. If they are passing thoughts, let them pass. If they are reoccurring thoughts, let them pass for now, but try to explore their source in a safe therapeutic environment. Don't assume that you have some dark evil nature just waiting to burst into action. Assume that you have *been* disturbed by a thought, not that you *are* disturbed for having it.

If you have experienced abuse as a child, *of course* you will have disturbing thoughts caused by memories or fears. You can accept the memories as part of your past without reenacting the behaviors as part of your future.

One of the darker sides of pornography is that it often includes disturbing or inappropriate images. If you can't escape the pull of pornography completely, try to choose images that at least pretend to be more about relationships than about shame or violence. Set a goal of finding "uplifting" pornography, about love and passion, then slowly wean yourself onto love stories that don't involve nude sex.

Finally, practice honesty, forgiveness, compassion and faith. Be honest with yourself and (if possible*) your significant other about your addiction and your efforts to let it go. Forgive yourself for your behavior. Forgive others for encouraging it, or shaming it, or introducing you to it, or whatever you need to forgive.

Try to experience compassion by humanizing the women in the pictures that you fantasize about. Try to imagine what kind of pain they must be in to be willing to debase themselves in this public way. Imagine their stories, from broken homes to abusive parents and vile boyfriends. See their anger. See their pain. See their search for identity. See their attempt to wrestle power from the chains of shame. Feel compassion for them, and the passion of lust will evaporate. They are participants in your drama. You victimize each other. Forgive them and yourself.

Have faith that you can take a different path. If you are a porn addict, you are still a child of the universe. You are still better known to the angels in heaven than you are to your own self. You were still loved by God before you were even created. The breath of the Holy Spirit was breathed into you, and you were created out of the clay of God's love. Nothing you have done or will do can ever change that.

The internet age has made it very difficult to escape pornography. The 24/7 availability of pictures and videos and the infinite variety of types of stimulation are unlike anything the world has seen before. If you continue to struggle with a porn addiction, or even if you are just curious about why internet porn is so much more addictive than magazines, then I encourage you to visit the website www.yourbrainonporn.com. It explains the science behind the effect of over stimulation on the brain and has pages and pages of great advice and support.

Some people have very strong feelings about pornography. It is often wise to wait until you are both in a therapeutic setting where these feelings can be explored safely before practicing this level of honesty. The more success and the less shame you have, the easier this honesty will be.

The M Word

Since I am on a roll, let me shock and anger some additional people by saying that masturbation is also not as big a deal as the ultra-religious would like us to believe. At the same time, it is not as completely harmless as the rest of the world would have us think.

Here's why: The *best* sex, as I explained earlier, is between two committed people who love each other and are expressing affection, intimacy, security, curiosity and a desire to please one another and grow closer together. Ideally, every association we have with sex will be connected to our loved one and be positive and ecstatic in nature, rather than being associated with shame, forbidden fruit, guilt or sin.

In an ideal world, people would enter marriage with knowledge, but with no sexual experience, and absolutely no negative thoughts, emotions, sensations or expectations around their sexuality, their private parts or their bodies in general.

Did you notice the word "ideal" at the beginning of that sentence? Unfortunately, we have ALL grown up with sex and shame intertwined more closely than any other two sensations. Because of this, the chance of a woman entering a marriage without any sexual experiences or associations is significantly reduced, and for a man, this may well seem to be impossible. (I'll explain the difference shortly.)

So, the question with masturbation is whether it increases or decreases the unhealthy relationship between sex and shame. The more experiences we have in which we associate sex, arousal and orgasm with shame or fear rather than affection, the more difficult it will be for us to turn off that association and replace it with something healthy.

This observation raises a host of additional questions that you will have to answer for yourself. No one else knows your history, your fantasies, your goals, your current relationship, or your desire or ability to transform your sex life.

For example, if you are currently one of the few people who associate sex with love and affection, and you associate masturbation with shame and secrecy, then masturbating will increase your association between sex and shame.

If, on the other hand, you associate sex with shame and sin, but you associate masturbation with self-care and have fantasies about love and affection, then masturbation might help change your attitude towards sex with your spouse and improve your love life.

If, like many, both sex and masturbation are associated with shame, and your sexual fantasies are fear, shame or intensity-based, then masturbation will just make it that much harder to develop an intimacy-based love life. On the other hand, if you can consciously change the nature of your fantasies, then you might be able to change the kind of sexual contact you are attracted to. After all, if we can change our spiritual attractions, we can change our fantasy attractions, too.

If this sound like a great excuse to continue masturbating, let me throw in this one word of caution: If your fantasies are too wonderful, then no real-life person will ever be able to match them. As Paul Simon said in "Kodachrome" – *"If you took all the girls I knew when I was single, and put them all together for one night. They would never match my sweet imagination. And everything looks worse in black and white."*

The *ideal*, then, is to have your fantasies and your reality, your expectations and your experience all be at the same time with the same person. But for many, the ideal is not even remotely possible. As they say, "That train left the station a long time ago."

For them, masturbation may well have a valid place as a tool for self-care. I really don't know. What I *think* I know is that actions are rarely moral or immoral. It is our motivation behind them and what we do with them that gives them meaning.

It's important to dispassionately consider how masturbation combined with a personal fantasy life might affect your current relationship, any potential future relationships, your feelings about yourself, your feelings about your religion, and the relationship between your heart, mind and body. Then make your peace with masturbation.

Whatever you decide to do, just don't shame yourself for the decision. Hold out for the ideal, or make do with what you can offer yourself. Then pay attention and remain open to change.

Why this issue is more difficult for men

Earlier I suggested that there is a difference between men and women in this area. People often disparage men for their constant interest in sex. One reason, as I mentioned, is that men respond more to visual stimulation, of which there is an abundance in our culture.

But there is another reason that is rarely talked about. A woman can go her entire lifetime and never experience an orgasm, but a man will start having an orgasm about once a month once he reaches puberty, whether he wants to or not. It is hard to miss something you've never had, but once you've experienced something pleasurable, it is difficult to ignore it.

Just as a woman ovulates every month, a man builds up a supply of semen that has to be released. If he doesn't release it through masturbation, it will be released in his sleep as a nocturnal emission (a wet dream). Because the body must be aroused to ejaculate, a male will usually wake up from a vivid dream in the throws of an orgasm. That dream, more often than not, will be of a sexual nature.

In other words, a healthy male will have a sexual fantasy resulting in an orgasm about once a month, whether he wants to or not. It is not surprising, then, that many men choose to assist the process consciously.

Wet dreams, like ovulation, are beyond a person's control and can therefore become a great source of confusion and shame. Like any dream, they are unpredictable. Sometimes they are about love and affection, but often they are about something intense, embarrassing or confusing. They are always messy. For boys, masturbating can be a way to take control of the experience, the feelings and the evidence. Like any pleasurable habit, it can be hard to break.

Women face a different challenge. If women were to have an orgasm every time they inserted a tampon, they would think about sex a lot more than they do. Instead, women who masturbate (and most do) get to take control of their sexuality in a way that men can't. It is a conscious choice, not an alternate to the unpredictable. It is a process of discovery rather than a required release.

Consequently, women tend to fantasize more about romance rather than sexual acts. If these fantasies help a woman learn about her body so that she can share more knowledgably with her spouse, then it may be a real blessing. If these fantasies are a way to escape intimacy with the person she ought to be closest to, then it can become a real problem. Only you know how you are using your intimate moments.

ASKING FOR HELP

I'm sorry. No matter how helpful I try to make this book, it will not be a substitute for a good therapist. I know that this will be disappointing to many of you, and absolutely terrifying for others. But if your life is not going as well as you would like, then finding an objective, compassionate person to consult with about it will do you a lot of good. It doesn't replace prayer and meditation, but then prayer and meditation don't replace consultation, either.

Having a real, live person look into your eyes and say, "You have a right to feel that way" can break through more layers of denial and fear than a hundred books, so give it a try.

Before I visited my first therapist, I was terrified. I was sure that she was going to call in the guys with the white coats and drag me away. Assuming that your fears are a little more rational than mine, let me start by relieving you of three of the most common.

First, there is the fear of stigma. If people know you are seeing a therapist, won't they think there is something wrong with you?

No. Not anyone worth paying any attention to, anyway. After all, if you don't think someone will be supportive of your efforts to improve your life, why would you bother to tell them you are in therapy? Your therapist won't tell them.

But you may be worried for nothing. If you have educated friends, then the chances are good that they, or one of their family members, have also seen a therapist at some point. We live in a stressful world. Between addictions and depression and work stress and family problems and ... well, there are thousands of good reasons to see a therapist. If you are ashamed of the *reason* why you need a therapist, then keep that part of it to yourself. That's your right.

The second fear is that it won't work. In the movies we see psychiatrists charging $200 an hour, week after week, while the client never seems to make any progress. First, forget everything you've ever seen about a therapist in any movie or TV show. They are *entertainment* and real, successful therapy sessions are not entertaining to watch. Real therapists would lose their licenses for doing what you see in the movies.

Consider therapy a kind of consultation on how to improve your life, the way you would bring a contractor in to help remodel your home. If you don't feel you are making progress after half a dozen sessions, *change therapists*. Don't give up. If a plumber did a bad job on your kitchen, you would get a new plumber, not order take-out for the rest of your life. If one therapist doesn't work well with you, there will be others to try. You deserve the best life possible, and finding the right "consultant" will help you do that.

Finally, people are afraid that therapy costs too much. Again, forget the movie version. Many therapists use a sliding scale based on what you can pay. Some take insurance (but don't decide how long to stay in therapy based on your insurance limit).

Also, if money is a big concern for you, then there is a good chance that your inner demons are sabotaging more than just your love life. The same shame and dysfunctional relationship patterns that are interfering with your serenity and psychological well-being are probably also interfering with your self-esteem and relationships at work. People who are psychologically and spiritually healthy are more successful in *every* aspect of their lives.

The year I started therapy was also the year I had to declare bankruptcy. I was living on about $12,000 a year, and considered buying a toothbrush a luxury. Therapy helped me change my relationship with money and wealth so that I was no longer ashamed *or afraid* to take care of myself materially. Of course, I can't *guarantee* that spending money on a therapist will pay for itself, but *can* pretty much guarantee that if you find a *good* therapist and *you do the work* you need to do, you will consider your money well spent.

Finding a Good Therapist

A "good" therapist is not the one that charges the most money, or the one with the most letters behind his or her name.

Good therapists hold healthy beliefs themselves and can confirm for you that they are true, not just in general, but *for you in specific.*

Here is a list of healthy beliefs that a good therapist will help you internalize:

I am safe—though my body may be frail and vulnerable, my soul is strong and eternal.

I am valuable—I matter to God and to the world. I make a difference.

I am lovable—I am created in the image of God and reflect spiritual virtues.

I am loving—I am attracted to the signs of God reflected in the people around me.

I have capacities—I am not a helpless pawn of the universe. I can make choices and accomplish goals.

I can grow—I am not static. I can learn and develop new skills and virtues.

A good therapist will also support your efforts at developing honesty, forgiveness, compassion and faith.

Before you walk into a therapist's office, you need to determine whether the therapist wants to focus on developing your spiritual capacity, or to simply change your brain chemistry and send you home. Does he or she believe the things I listed above? If therapists don't believe these things themselves, they may not have the tools needed to help you counteract your own unhealthy beliefs.

If you believe in God, Free Will and the importance of spiritual growth, then you need a therapist who can do more than smile condescendingly at you while writing a prescription. In short, you need a therapist who understands that you were born with an innate longing for God, and who shares that longing.

Fortunately, there are thousands of spiritually-minded therapists who, if given the opportunity, will be happy to support a process of healing that includes respect for your spiritual development. I have found that non-denominational Pastoral Counselors are the most open to an integrated psychological *and* spiritual approach to healing, but there are also spiritually-minded social workers, psychologists, psychiatrists and a dozen different forms of certified therapists. Many therapists and treatment programs use a twelve-step recovery approach to personal issues. Their focus on a "Higher Power" offers a non-denominational yet spiritual approach to healing. While counselors' training is valuable, it is their ability to make the personal connection that will make the healing possible.

If you are hesitant to ask friends and family for recommendations, then you can still find out a lot about a prospective therapist before seeing them. These days you can go online and research a therapist's training and philosophy. Look at their photographs. Read what they have to say about themselves and their style. Notice the words they use. Listen to your intuition, then e-mail or call for a trial appointment.

In Conclusion

I am hoping I can end this book with a bang, but that is really up to you.

- In *The Secret of Emotions*, I explain that our emotions tell us about the presence or absence of virtues in our lives.
- In *4 Tools of Emotional Healing*, I explain the value of developing honesty, forgiveness, compassion and faith.
- In *Longing for Love*, I define love not as a sensation, but as an attraction to the attributes of God reflected in the hearts of the people around us.
- I explain that healthy relationships are the result of falling in love with virtues, and then letting that love lead you to people who are of good character.
- I offer hope that each of us is capable of retraining our hearts to become attracted to the qualities that create healthy relationships.
- I point towards the means of identifying virtues and becoming attracted to them.
- I describe the many emotions that masquerade as love.
- I explain the difference between intensity and intimacy and argue that they are mutually exclusive.

- I give reasons why you should choose intimacy over intensity.
- I offer insights into how to deal with feelings of loneliness and anxiety.
- I point out some love myths—like signs and soul mates—that create chaos.
- I encourage you to be happy with the one you love.
- I shine a light on temptation in order to increase clarity and reduce shame.
- I remind you that you are defined by your relationship to God, not your sexual attractions.
- I encourage you to accept professional help and support.

Any one of these pieces of insight would have saved me years of heartache and shame if it had been offered to me when I was younger. Whether it can be of any use to you is entirely in your hands.

Good luck.

About the Author

Justice Saint Rain is the author of several books that blend psychology with spiritual insights. He is both a writer and an artist, and has been producing a line of spiritually-oriented material for over 30 years. He currently lives with his family on a farm in Southern Indiana.

He does not do life-coaching or consultations by phone or e-mail, but he does have a FaceBook page called *Love, Lust and the Longing for God*, an author's page at GoodReads.com and a writer's blog.

He will be happy to try to answer questions and respond to comments posted at any of these sites.

Join the conversation at:
www.justicesaintrain.com

Love Lust and the Longing for God is available as three separate gift books, or as a single volume for personal use:
The Secret of Emotions
4 Tools of Emotional Healing
Longing for Love
Love, Lust and the Longing for God

Available in print and Kindle editions from:
SecretofEmotions.com and Amazon.com

Made in the USA
Charleston, SC
25 February 2013